# Education for Innovation and Independent Learning

# Education for Innovation and Independent Learning

Ronaldo Mota
David Scott

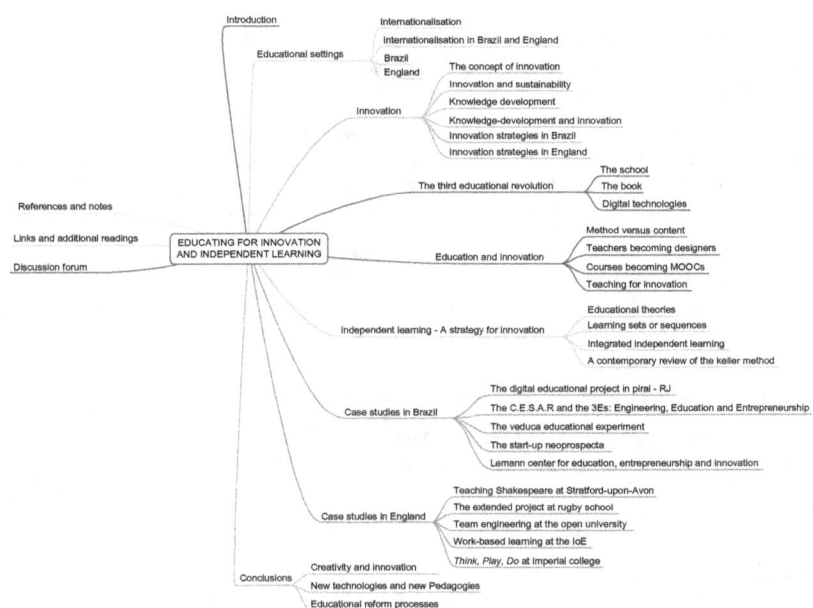

AMSTERDAM • BOSTON • HEIDELBERG • LONDON • NEW YORK • OXFORD
PARIS • SAN DIEGO • SAN FRANCISCO • SINGAPORE • SYDNEY • TOKYO

Elsevier
The Boulevard, Langford Lane, Kidlington, Oxford, OX5 1GB, UK
225 Wyman Street, Waltham, MA 02451, USA

First published 2014

Copyright © 2014 Elsevier Inc. All rights reserved
© 2013 Elsevier Editora Ltda.

This edition of Educando Para Inovação e Aprendizagem Independente by Mota and Scott is published by arrangement with Elsevier Editora Ltda. of Rua Sete de Setembro, 111, 16° andar, 20050-006 Rio de Janeiro, RJ, Brazil

No part of this publication may be reproduced or transmitted in any form or by any means, electronic or mechanical, including photocopying, recording, or any information storage and retrieval system, without permission in writing from the publisher. Details on how to seek permission, further information about the Publisher's permissions policies and our arrangement with organizations such as the Copyright Clearance Center and the Copyright Licensing Agency, can be found at our website: www.elsevier.com/permissions.

This book and the individual contributions contained in it are protected under copyright by the Publisher (other than as may be noted herein).

**Notices**
Knowledge and best practice in this field are constantly changing. As new research and experience broaden our understanding, changes in research methods, professional practices, or medical treatment may become necessary.

Practitioners and researchers must always rely on their own experience and knowledge in evaluating and using any information, methods, compounds, or experiments described herein. In using such information or methods they should be mindful of their own safety and the safety of others, including parties for whom they have a professional responsibility.

To the fullest extent of the law, neither the Publisher nor the authors, contributors, or editors, assume any liability for any injury and/or damage to persons or property as a matter of products liability, negligence or otherwise, or from any use or operation of any methods, products, instructions, or ideas contained in the material herein.

**British Library Cataloguing-in-Publication Data**
A catalogue record for this book is available from the British Library

**Library of Congress Cataloging-in-Publication Data**
A catalog record for this book is available from the Library of Congress

ISBN: 978-0-12-800847-8

For information on all Elsevier publications
visit our website at store.elsevier.com

This book has been manufactured using Print On Demand technology. Each copy is produced to order and is limited to black ink. The online version of this book will show color figures where appropriate.

# DEDICATION

*It is usual to dedicate the book to the family members, and, for sure, they deserve, always.....*

*Nevertheless, this time, the authors decided to dedicate not to individuals, but to the place where the individuals live, or lived, creatively...*

*The authors dedicate this book to London, the exact environment to conjugate innovation with education.*

# CONTENTS

List of Figures ................................................................................. ix
List of Tables .................................................................................. xi
Acknowledgements ....................................................................... xiii
Foreword ....................................................................................... xv

**Chapter 1  Introduction** ............................................................... 1

**Chapter 2  Educational Settings** ................................................. 5
2.1   Internationalization ................................................................ 5
2.2   Education in Brazil and England ............................................ 8
Notes ............................................................................................. 19

**Chapter 3  Innovation** ................................................................. 21
3.1   The Concept of Innovation ................................................... 21
3.2   Innovation and Sustainability ............................................... 25
3.3   Knowledge-development ...................................................... 26
3.4   Knowledge-development and Innovation ............................ 31
3.5   Innovation Strategies in Brazil ............................................. 34
3.6   Innovation Strategies in England .......................................... 37
Notes ............................................................................................. 40

**Chapter 4  The Third Educational Revolution** ........................ 41
4.1   The School ............................................................................ 43
4.2   The Book .............................................................................. 48
4.3   Digital Technologies ............................................................. 50
Note ............................................................................................... 54

**Chapter 5  Education and Innovation** ...................................... 55
5.1   Curriculum Matters ............................................................... 58
5.2   Teachers as Designers .......................................................... 61
5.3   Massive Open Online Courses ............................................. 65
5.4   Teaching for Innovation ....................................................... 68
Notes ............................................................................................. 71

## Chapter 6 Independent Learning: A Strategy for Innovation ............... 73
6.1 Learning Theories ....................................................................... 76
6.2 Learning Frameworks ................................................................. 81
6.3 Learning Sets or Sequences ........................................................ 85
6.4 Independent Learning ................................................................. 89
6.5 Digital Teaching and Learning Approaches ............................... 90
6.6 Learning Skills ............................................................................ 94
Notes ..................................................................................................... 94

## Chapter 7 Case Studies in Brazil ..................................................... 97
7.1 The Digital Educational Project in Piraí-RJ ............................. 101
7.2 C.E.S.A.R. and the 3Es: Engineering, Education
    and Entrepreneurship ................................................................ 104
7.3 The Veduca Educational Experiment ....................................... 107
7.4 Start-up Neoprospecta .............................................................. 109
7.5 The Lemann Center for Educational Entrepreneurship
    and Innovation .......................................................................... 113
Notes ................................................................................................... 116

## Chapter 8 Case Studies in England ............................................... 117
8.1 Teaching Shakespeare at Stratford-upon-Avon ........................ 117
8.2 The Extended Project at Rugby ................................................ 120
8.3 Team Engineering at the Open University ............................... 126
8.4 Word-based Learning at the Institute of Education ................. 129
8.5 *Think, Play and Do* at Imperial College ................................. 133
Notes ................................................................................................... 135

## Chapter 9 Conclusions ..................................................................... 137
9.1 Creativity and Innovation ......................................................... 139
9.2 New Technologies and New Pedagogies .................................. 142
9.3 Educational Reform Processes ................................................. 146
Note ..................................................................................................... 148

**References** ........................................................................................ 149
**Index** ................................................................................................. 155

# LIST OF FIGURES

Figure 1.1    Medieval copy of a book by Gautier de Metz/1463.    4
"L'image du Monde". Detail of a miniature of a master and scholars. This figure is under Public Domain by Wikimedia Commons. As can be seen at: http://commons.wikimedia.org/wiki/File:Master_and_scholars_-_1464_-_L%27image_du_Monde.jpg. Accessed January 2013.

Figure 2.1    Drawing by P. G. Bertichem/1856. "Colégio Pedro    11
II and Church of San Joaquim." This figure is under Public Domain by Wikimedia Commons. As can be seen at: http://commons.wikimedia.org/wiki/File:Bertichen_colegio_pedro_ii_igreja_s_joaquim_.jpg. Accessed January 2013.

Figure 2.2    Teacher training and students at the Institute of    16
Education, University of London, 1946. Mr J G Anquandah from Accra, Gold Coast, tells a story to a group of 5-year-olds at Marlborough Infants School in Isleworth, as part of his training at the Institute of Education. The rest of the class can be seen, continuing with their work at desks behind them. According to the original caption, Mr Anquandah was a student at the Accra Government Training College, and won the Gold Coast Teacher's Certificate. He was headmaster of a large infant school in Accra and is taking a special course in Infant-Junior work at the Institute. This figure is under Public Domain by Wikimedia Commons. As can be seen at: http://commons.wikimedia.org/wiki/File:Colonial_Students_in_Great_Britain-_Students_at_University_of_London_Institute_of_Education,_London,_England,_UK,_1946_D29306.jpg?uselang = en-gb. Accessed May 2013.

Figure 3.1    Work by Eugène Grasset/2012. "A translation    22
from *Methode de Composition Ornamentale*".

|  |  |  |
|---|---|---|
| | This figure is under Public Domain by Wikimedia Commons. As can be seen at: http://commons.wikimedia.org/wiki/File:Grasset-ctg-poster-innovation.jpg. Accessed January 2013. | |
| Figure 3.2 | Knowledge-Development management scheme. | 33 |
| Figure 3.3 | Science-Technology-Innovation time-sequenced in accordance with the traditional and linear relationship. | 33 |
| Figure 3.4 | Science-Technology-Innovation time-sequenced in accordance with the contemporary and circular relationship. | 33 |
| Figure 4.1 | Fresco by Rafaello Sanzio/151. "The School of Athens". This figure is under Public Domain by Wikimedia Commons. As can be seen at: http://commons.wikimedia.org/wiki/File:Diogenes_-_La_scuola_di_Atene.jpg. Accessed January 2013. | 45 |
| Figure 4.2 | "Printing Press, sixteenth century in Germany". In: Tolnai világtörténelme. Ujkor-könyv, book. By Tolnai korabeli kép alapján (Gottfried-Történelmi krónika) (1908). This figure is under Public Domain by Wikimedia Commons. As seen at: http://commons.wikimedia.org/wiki/File:Nyomda_16._sz-Tolnai.jpg. Accessed January 2013. | 50 |
| Figure 5.1 | Stained glass window by Louis Comfort Tiffany (1890), located in Linsly-Chittenden Hall at Yale University. "Education". This figure is under Public Domain by Wikimedia Commons. As can be seen at: http://commons.wikimedia.org/wiki/File:Tiffany_Education.JPG. Accessed January 2013. | 56 |
| Figure 6.1 | Oil on canvas by Krzysztof Lubieniecki/1717. "School-teacher". This figure is under Public Domain by Wikimedia Commons. As can be seen at: http://commons.wikimedia.org/wiki/File:Lubieniecki_School-teacher.jpg. Accessed January 2013. | 92 |
| Figure 7.1 | Neoprospecta logo. Authorised by the company. | 110 |
| Figure 8.1 | Photograph of Rugby School, where the Rugby sport was invented. Photo given by the *Rugby School*. | 121 |
| Figure 8.2 | Curricular modes in a continuum. | 124 |

# LIST OF TABLES

Table 4.1  Three Educational Revolutions and their Principal Characteristics  44

Table 5.1  Comparison between Innovative and Traditional Didactic Pedagogic Modes  62

# ACKNOWLEDGEMENTS

This book is based upon work supported by the Coordenação de Aperfeiçoamento de Pessoal de Nível Superior (Brazilian Agency CAPES), through Cátedra Anísio Teixeira, a joint initiative with the Institute of Education, University of London (IoE). We recognize that this book would not have been possible without the participation of CAPES and IoE, and we express our gratitude to them.

We would like to thank Alice Carraturi, Andreia Inamorato, Berenice Roth, Gabriel Goldmeier, Fernanda Furuno, Hélio Chaves Filho, Juliana Bertazzo, João Fernando Gomes de Oliveira (especially about innovation and sustainability), Luiz Fabio Mesquiati, Maria Cowen, Newton Padilha and Nina Roth Mota, for taking time out from their busy schedules to serve as preliminary readers.

Finally, we would like to thank our families for the support they provided us, without whose love and encouragement, we would not have finished this book.

http://www.educatingforinnovation.com

# FOREWORD

In the past, it was possible to say that "educational innovation" corresponded to an oxymoron, as the vision regarding the role of formal learning was to prepare new generations of students for their future through the study of the past; a concept that now needs to be modified. Matthew Arnold (1822–1888) argued eloquently that the study of the "best that has been thought of and said" so far in the world would be the ideal platform for the cultural development of citizens faced with the anarchy that accompanies industrialization, materialism and individualism produced by modern society.

Could it be that, in various corners of the world, street demonstrations, especially involving violence, represent evidence of the inadequacy of educational systems (in those countries where they are triggered), for being unable to find the "optimal dosage"; that is, the appropriate balance between traditional cultural teaching (Arnold's dream) and innovative and dynamic teaching, that develops close links between contemporary society (and its requirements) and educational institutions?

Tension about the perpetuatation of the legacy of the past is common, provided that it innovates for the present and the future. However, we might ask why the educational world is so late in the adoption of the tools and benefits of digital technologies, as they were notably expropriated decades ago by the worlds of finance, industry and medicine. Excessive conservatism? An example of an ostrich-effect? Or inadequate leadership? Whatever the cause, or causes, it is now impossible to ignore the delay and its consequences.

This work by Mota and Scott is a "territorial mapping" of learning. Far from being encyclopaedic or composing an exhaustive list of cases in the two countries that they focus on, they provide a very clear and succinct review of the best and main ideas that were important in the last century, but are still significant. Through a discussion whose high level of abstraction can cover jurisdictional, disciplinary and diverse educational levels, the rich summary covering a subject as complex as "learning" is of great value. Reading this part of the book, an attempt at marking boundaries, allows a trained professional in fields other than education, but who might want to become a teacher, to understand current ideas and theories circulating about learning, many of them in conflict. The study of this content will also allow educators to identify contradictions, discrepancies and gaps in their own current practices, thus justifying their attempts to innovate through experimentation with new solutions.

Mota and Scott do not mince words, and make no attempt to please the supporters of different schools of educational thought; nor do they give voice to the known "myths of innovation", which suggest that innovation followers produce their actions with the help of "epiphanies" or "divine manifestations", or another myth that claims as innovation only those proposals created by solitary individuals, without the support of others. They define innovation as "the application of ideas that are successful"; they also suggest that the innovation process goes through several stages, briefly described by the authors. Similarly, they propose an interesting model for teaching innovation, which is similar to design, citizenship and skills teaching approaches that are now more commonly used today.

Perhaps the practice of "educational innovation" (common-place and centuries-old in England) that is mostly missing in Brazil is "independent learning", which, with the advent of digital technologies, points to the importance of asynchronous communication and "intelligent" systems (which may be able, for example, to correct and qualitatively evaluate student work without human interference). The idea of "independent learning" is growing in importance. Learning independently, with the support of resources available on the web, and then to sit exams to gain the certification of the acquired knowledge, skills and attitudes, always represents democratic progress for millions of people. This learning profile will contribute to the creation of a national workforce which is larger and better qualified in the case of Brazil, where this modality is subordinated to the category of EJA-Youth and Adults (people over 18 years of age, studying at primary and secondary school level at a later age).

In short, this book offers to an extensive and diverse audience a thorough presentation of knowledge of the past, the present and the future in relation to learning. Written with exceptional clarity and elegance, its content will certainly inspire those interested in education to look for new solutions to typical, generic and specific problems, well identified in this study. For this, and on behalf of future readers, I thank the authors.

**Fredric M. Litto**
*Emeritus Professor of the University of São Paulo, Member of the Executive Committee of the International Council for Open and Distance Learning, and President of the Brazilian Association of Distance Education-ABED*

# CHAPTER 1

# Introduction

*The future is not something that will happen, the future is what is happening now*
**(Gary Hamel and C.K. Prahalad, 1994)**

Our principal concern in this book is to understand three important ideas: learning, technology and innovation, and to examine these ideas and the relationships between them *in situ*; that is, we examine a number of cases of learning technologies in action in two countries, England and Brazil. The purpose of our study is to provide an explanation of the means to, and constraints on, improvements to educational policies and practices, with particular reference to innovation. We have a plethora of theoretical models that, in attempting to deal with causal relations, usually come to the conclusion that there are socio-economic-cultural constraints, but these observations largely remain at an abstract level and/or come to very general conclusions that are not of particular help to practitioners in the field. These issues can only be properly addressed after examining the empirical reality and having a spectrum of cases to analyse. By combining the theoretical and the practical, our aim is to explain how and under what conditions new modes of learning can be put into practice successfully and sustainably, in order for the learner to develop innovatory skills and dispositions for work and in his or her life course.

We begin by introducing the principal themes of the book and then argue for a productive relationship between innovation, technology and pedagogy. In addition to explaining the argument which runs through the whole book, this introductory chapter will also provide an account of the book's contents.

In Chapter 2 we introduce and discuss the central purposes of *international education*. These are: developing citizens of the world in relation to culture, language and the capacity to live among people of other nations; building and reinforcing a sense of identity and cultural awareness; fostering recognition and development of universal human values; stimulating curiosity and inquiry in order to develop a spirit of discovery and enjoyment of learning; equipping students with the skills to learn and acquire knowledge, individually or collaboratively; and providing an international context for responding to local requirements and interests.

The introduction of an international dimension in educational institutions has important consequences for students, teachers and researchers. It is a phenomenon that is increasingly influencing the way we teach and learn, and thus requires the development of new methodologies. The introduction of technological innovations *stricto sensu* and innovations *lato sensu* as key elements for social and economic development is defining the way we rethink the educational process in a world where preparing people for innovation is becoming increasingly important. In the chapter we examine the characteristics of the two educational settings that form the backdrop to this study: Brazil and England.

In Chapter 3 we look at the concept of *innovation*, a key concept in the formation of modern societies. In the middle ages this meant novelty arising from human creativity; whereas today it has become emblematic of modern societies and directly associated with the possibility of sustainable economic and social development. The concept of innovation is broader than simply technological innovation. More recently, a new wave of innovation approaches such as *open innovation, democratizing innovation, creative economies* and *organizational and marketing innovation* have been introduced. Many of these are associated with new types of knowledge production such as workplaces and homes, rather than traditional research laboratories and universities.

In Chapter 4 we examine the importance of innovation in contemporary society and the available new technologies that can be used in education. We suggest that we are entering the third *educational revolution*, which implies that substantial changes are needed to the traditional ways we use to teach and learn, as well as to how knowledge is produced and disseminated. We are now in a world where it is becoming clearer than ever that, despite the essential roles that traditional education systems have played, standard solutions and approaches are not appropriate for meeting new educational and social needs.

In Chapter 5 we analyse the relationship between *education and innovation*. This is a complex and rich theme, especially with respect to the impact of new technologies. To better understand the incorporation of digital technologies in the classroom, it is perhaps helpful to remember previous promises and false expectations, as well as the successes and achievements of the older cousins of last century's "digital technologies", such as movies, radio and television. It is also worth noting that it is a characteristic of technology-based education in general to place the learner at the centre of the learning process. This allows him or her to have some input into the contents and sequences of the learning process, and thus more independence and greater control over it. We therefore address the complex but important notion of independent learning.

In Chapter 6 we develop a *theory of learning*, one moreover which takes account of the principal themes of the book: developing new learning technologies, and developing innovatory life-styles. One characteristic of a world where innovation is central is the role played by new technologies, especially digital, including the internet. They have the advantage of allowing the student, as well as the teacher, to develop his or her learning beyond the physical environment of the classroom, thus widening access to education. Even so, we need to be careful about exaggerating the claims made for technological innovations and adopt a more circumspect approach to education and technology. In this case, the term *technology* refers to far more than just machinery and artifacts—it now also refers to social contexts and circumstances.

In Chapters 7 and 8 we examine a variety of cases of new pedagogic and technological approaches. In Brazil, our cases include: The Digital Educational Project in Piraí-RJ; The C.E.S.A.R. and the Engineering, Education and Entrepreneurship Project; The Veduca Educational Experiment; Start-up Neoprospecta; and the Lemann Center for Education, Entrepreneurship and Innovation. In England, our cases comprise: Teaching Shakespeare at Stratford-upon-Avon; The Extended Project at Rugby School; Team Engineering at the Open University; Work-based Learning at the Institute of Education, University of London; and *Think, Play and Do* at Imperial College London.

In the final chapter, we bring together the three essential components discussed in the book: pedagogy, technology and innovation, and draw some conclusions about the relationships between them. Education has traditionally contributed to individual learning, the

4  Education for Innovation and Independent Learning

*Figure 1.1 Medieval copy of a book by Gautier de Metz/1463. "L'image du Monde". Detail of a miniature of a master and scholars.*

common good and national prosperity. The world is changing and education has to change with it, even if at the moment its approaches, technologies and outputs are outdated, and increasingly unable to cope with the need for innovation in society (see Figure 1.1). This book attempts to make connections between education, technology and innovation in the contemporary world.

# CHAPTER 2

# Educational Settings

*If we teach today's students as we taught yesterday's, we rob them of their future*

**(John Dewey, 1944)**

In this chapter we identify the characteristics of educational environments that allow learning to take place and is directed towards the promotion of sustainable futures. The United Nations Educational, Scientific and Cultural Organization (UNESCO)[1] have suggested that these include: (i) a willingness to investigate issues in the local, school, and wider community; (ii) a readiness to recognize social, economic, ecological and political dimensions of issues needed to resolve them; and (iii) the ability to analyse issues and to participate in actions aimed at achieving a sustainable future. A principal concern in citizenship education is the development of these skills for active democratic citizenship roles, and as one of the defining features of a sustainable society[2].

The introduction of an international dimension into school and university institutions reaches beyond individual students, teachers and researchers. It emanates from a need to respond to new demands coming from a globalized society that is increasingly moderating the way we teach and learn, and therefore requires new methodologies to be developed. The importance of technological innovations, both *stricto sensu* and *lato sensu*, as key elements for social and economic development, is central to a rethinking of educational processes in a world where preparing people for an innovatory culture is considered by some to be of central importance.

## 2.1 INTERNATIONALIZATION

Internationalization in education has, as its primary purpose, the preparation of the academic community, comprising students, teachers and researchers, and those engaged in entrepreneurial activities, for successful participation in an increasingly globalized and interdependent world. Successful international education strategies consist of specific approaches and pedagogies at different levels: institutional, national and sectorial. Why is the development of processes of internationalization and globalization of educational systems and mechanisms considered to be so important? As the world becomes smaller and as nation states become more closely aligned with each other, economic, scientific and technological competitiveness becomes a central element in the global economy.

Technological innovations, especially the emergence of digital technologies and the development of multi-modal forms of expression, are influencing the construction of new educational environments. The growing middle class culture in many countries around the world is creating unprecedented demand for educational services from both private and public suppliers. The number of people entering higher education has increased exponentially over the past decade, with the result that between the years 2000 and 2010 the proportion of adults worldwide who have received tertiary education rose from 19% to 29%, and all reasonable estimates suggest that this trend will continue.

Goddard (2012) estimates that the number of students around the world enrolled in higher education will reach 262 million by 2025, up from 178 million in 2010. In particular, three countries are primarily responsible for the increase in numbers: China (26%), India (18%) and Brazil (14%). Private sector provision for higher education across most of Latin America has increased, with this trend reflected in other parts of the world, particularly in Asia. How these countries will rapidly expand their higher education systems while ensuring that private institutions deliver good quality teaching and learning environments is a key question. One of the consequences of the internationalization process is that opportunities for the educational private sector to expand will grow broader and deeper, because, some have suggested, this sector is able to respond more quickly than the public sector to demand for services and improved travel and communications technologies.

Internationalizing higher education has recently become a global phenomenon. Goddard (2012) suggests that the number of internationally mobile students is expected to almost double to 8 million by 2025. The benefits of this process include increased funding and powerful global alumni links for institutions, access to high-quality and culturally diverse education for students, and skilled-migrant streams for governments. To achieve such goals, universities and colleges have been developing international programmes, taught in the home institution and abroad. They include internationalizing their curricula, redefining their mission statements to embrace an international dimension, building into their policy documents targets for recruitment of international students and staff, and developing programmes and practices that meet the needs of international students (Knight, 1994).

With regards to international student mobility, the International Baccalaureate (IB) Foundation, established in Switzerland at the end of the 1960s, prepares students for international higher education through the development of a curriculum and diploma qualification recognized by universities around the world (Bunnell, 2010). The IB Foundation has identified eight criteria for international education[3]: (i) developing citizens of the world in relation to culture, language and capacity to live among people of other nations; (ii) building and reinforcing students' sense of identity and cultural awareness; (iii) fostering student's recognition and development of universal human values; (iv) stimulating curiosity and inquiry in order to foster a spirit of discovery and enjoyment of learning; (v) equipping students with the skills to learn and acquire knowledge, individually or collaboratively, and to apply these skills and knowledge accordingly across a broad range of areas; (vi) providing international content whilst responding to local requirements and interests; (vii) encouraging diversity and flexibility in teaching methods; and (viii) providing appropriate forms of assessment and international benchmarking.

In relation to this last criterion, Yemini (2012) has proposed that school-based internationalization should have the following goals: (i) evaluating teachers', students' and other stakeholders' opinions, attitudes and beliefs in a range of learning opportunities; (ii) monitoring internationalization activities in schools according to the proposed framework together with validity studies; (iii) mapping the gaps in teacher training in order to identify and develop generic skills and competencies related to internationalization; (iv) expanding this course of study in the context of different populations in developed and developing countries; (v) providing a secondary analysis of schools with different levels of internationalization to identify parameters that assist and encourage this phenomenon; and (vi) completing a long-term follow-up of students and teachers to track transformations in their views of internationalization.

## 2.2 EDUCATION IN BRAZIL AND ENGLAND

In the second half of this book we identify and examine a series of pedagogical projects relating to innovation and educational reforms in two countries, Brazil and England. Although each of these countries provides a unique context for education reform, we would argue that the success or otherwise of any pedagogical innovation is context-bound. We also want to suggest that policy and practice transfers between different jurisdictions, nations and educational environments are both possible and desirable. However, in the first place this requires a full or complete understanding of those factors that allow an innovatory pedagogical practice to become embedded in the system.

There are two plausible theories of policy borrowing and policy transfer. Policy borrowing in our first variant ($P_1$) has a series of stages, as in the model developed by Philips and Schweisfurth (2008): conceptualization (neutralizing the questions to be addressed), contextualization (providing a description of the issues against local backgrounds in two or more of the cases), isolation of differences (determining variances), explanation (developing an hypothesis), reconceptualization (contextualizing the findings), and application (generalizing the findings). This model can be usefully amended (i.e., to $P_2$) so that it now includes seven steps or phases. The first step is where the investigator conceptualizes the focus of the investigation. The second step is when a mechanism is identified within Country A (where this is the country from which the policy is being borrowed). The third step is understanding how this mechanism works in the context of Country A; in other words, identifying those factors within Country A which allow the mechanism to work as it was intended or at least as it has been adapted to a new set of circumstances (over time but still within Country A). The fourth step is identifying another country (B), which seems to be a suitable recipient of this mechanism; that is, it seems to have some similarities to the donor's context. The fifth step is identifying those similarities and differences between the contexts of the two countries. The sixth step is making a judgement about the degree of similarity and difference between the two settings and subsequently making a judgement about the amount and type of change required for the mechanism to work in Country B, which also requires a judgement to be made about whether the mechanism is working or not; this involves predicting how one mechanism that seems to work in one particular socio-historical setting should work in another which is characterized by a different set of structures. And finally, having identified the consequences of transferring the mechanism to the new country, the policy transfer is implemented.

The first task in both of these models is to provide a full description of the characteristics of these two countries of origin, that is, the countries from which the policy or practice originated. In short, what are the characteristics of the typical educational environments found in these two countries? And what clues might these give us as to why these technological pedagogic innovations were successful in their original environments?

### 2.2.1 Brazil

The Brazilian federation comprises the Union, 26 States, the Federal District and 5,564 Municipalities in an area covering 8.5 million km$^2$, which represents almost half of the territory of South America. In terms of education, the Union (Federal Government), States (and Federal District) and Municipalities collaborate to organize their respective education systems and the Union may supplement the efforts of each unit of the federation, if required.

Following the Brazilian Law 9394/96[4], named as *Directives and Framework for the Education Sector*, each state of the Federation has its own education system and authorities (Education Councils/Secretariats). In addition, each municipality may or may not integrate the education system of the respective state. Each member of the federation provides for all levels of the education system, but the Federal Government prioritizes higher education and technological education, the states prioritize secondary schools (from grades 10–12), and the municipalities are required to prioritize the provision of primary (grades 1–9) and secondary education. There is a National Council of Education[5], responsible for setting guidelines for a common minimum curriculum for primary and secondary education, with detailed curricula set by the states and municipalities. It is nationally established that the following subjects are compulsory: Portuguese, Mathematics, Science, Social Studies, Art, at least one Modern Foreign Language, and Philosophy and Sociology—this last is only for secondary schools.

The Brazilian population of almost 200 million inhabitants is mainly concentrated in the Southeast and Northeast regions, which represent approximately 43% and 28% of the total population, respectively. It is important to note that younger people, between 0 and 39 years of age, represent approximately 68% of the total[6]. The Brazilian age structure has changed over the last two decades, as a consequence of the reduction in the mortality and birth rates, as well as the enhancement of the population's life span. Following the global trend, an intense industrialization process occurred between the 1950s and the 1980s, with the result that the urban population quickly surpassed the rural one by the end of the 1960s, so that today the urban population represents more than 85% of the overall population.

The Brazilian government has identified a series of key educational policies for the period of 2010–2020[7]: raising teacher quality; protecting the early development of the most vulnerable children; building a world-class secondary education system; maximizing the impact of federal policy on basic education; and exploring the links between innovation and education.

In education, even though considerable progress has been made, Brazil is still falling behind the average learning levels of other middle-income countries. For instance, Brazil is not as advanced as Chile, Uruguay and Mexico in Latin American countries (cf., Santos, 2011). Figure 2.1 is an example of an early College of Education, developed through an association with the established Church in Brazil.

Brazil's progress has been in part due to the massive expansion of schooling in the country over the last 15 years, and more recently to the quality targets that the federal government, in partnership with states and municipalities, has established, along with the provision of appropriate resources. The Brazilian Educational Development Plan[8], launched by the Ministry of Education in 2007, has implemented a number of action programmes to enhance the quality of education. Among them are: a digital inclusion programme whose aims include the installation of microcomputers and multimedia laboratories in all public schools; and the production of multimedia digital content to support schools and students by creating an educational portal called the Teacher's Portal (*Portal do Professor*)[9]. In this context, the Brazilian Open University (in Portuguese: *Universidade Aberta do Brasil*, UAB)[10]

*Figure 2.1 Drawing by P.G. Bertichem/1856:* Colégio Pedro II and Church of San Joaquim.

was also launched, which offers teacher training programmes and other educational programmes to a range of learners, allowing teachers and learners increased access to digital resources, and educational content in a variety of formats (Mota, 2008; Mota and Chaves, 2006).

There are three types of higher education institutions in Brazil: Schools (*Faculdades*), Colleges (*Centros Universitários*) and Universities (*Universidades*). The first type only offers a narrow range of courses and is the least autonomous of the three. The second one, created in 1997, offers many courses, although its curriculum is relatively limited and these colleges operate autonomously in their respective municipalities. The universities are multi-disciplinary institutions, with an obligation to do research, and teach at undergraduate and postgraduate (Master's and Doctoral) levels[11]. At around the middle of the last century, Brazil decided that it had to develop a network of public universities, associated with research and offering postgraduate courses, in order to prepare more teachers for the expanding university system (Mota, 2013). At least one federal university was built in each state while, at the same time, thousands of students were sent abroad to enroll on Master's and

Doctorate degree programmes. On their return to Brazil in the 1970s, research groups were formed and hundreds of postgraduate programmes were launched—this contributed to the massive expansion of postgraduate education in Brazil.

Brazil has experienced considerable growth in the number of higher education institutions over the last two decades, including private institutions (Mota, 2007, 2011). This spread of higher education in Brazil was achieved through active state support to provide equitable opportunities of higher education for everyone and it has been a proclaimed policy of the government to also encourage private investment in higher education. Whilst research universities have largely been in the public domain, supported directly by the Federal or State Governments, Brazil has had a history of having large numbers of colleges established and maintained by private management. In recent times, the private self-financing institutions, colleges and other degree awarding institutions, have gained prominence. In accordance with the 2012 higher education census[12], Brazil has around 6.7 million undergraduate enrolments, of which three-quarters are in the private sector; in total, there are 2,377 institutions, with 278 public (99 from federal, 108 from states and 71 from municipalities' institutions) and 2,099 private.

The higher education system in Brazil has been organized according to the European (mainly France and Italy) and American traditions of academic schools, with the first universities established during the 1930s. Even so, in spite of the recent expansion, only about 14% of the age cohort (18–24 years) is enrolled. Public higher education is free of fees, but enrols fewer than 25% of the students[12]. The quality of provision is very uneven, both in public and private institutions, with a concentration of scientific research among the public universities, even though private sector universities have become more active players in this area recently. For a country with a developing economy and only substantial recent investment in higher education, Brazil had an impressive number of universities in the 2012 QS World University Rankings®[13]; many of which have climbed up the rankings significantly in recent years. In the QS World University Rankings 2011/12, Brazil's highest-ranked university was the *Universidade de São Paulo* (USP) at 169; a position it shares with Mexico's *Universidad Nacional Autónoma de México* (UNAM). Next was the *Universidade Estadual de Campinas* (Unicamp), ranked 235, which is also based in the São Paulo area.

It is interesting to observe that both USP and Unicamp universities have moved up significantly between the 2010 and 2011 rankings, climbing an impressive 84 places and 57 places, respectively. Also featuring in the global rankings in 2011/12 were the *Universidade Federal do Rio de Janeiro* (381), *Universidade Federal de São Paulo* (446) and *Universidade Federal de Minas Gerais* (501). Other Brazilian universities listed and also on the rise, are: *Universidade Estadual Paulista "Júlio de Mesquita Filho", Universidade Federal do Rio Grande do Sul, Pontifícia Universidade Católica do Rio de Janeiro, Universidade de Brasilia, Universidade Federal de Santa Catarina* and *Universidade Federal de São Carlos*.

Unsurprisingly, given its strong global presence, Brazil dominates the QS regional rankings for Latin America. In the 2012 QS University Rankings: Latin America™[14], Brazil had more than a quarter of the region's top 250 universities. This included three universities in the top ten, with *Universidade de São Paulo* ranked as the leading university in Latin America for the second year running, followed by *Unicamp* (third) and *Universidade Federal do Rio de Janeiro* (eighth).

The country has the most prominent system of postgraduate studies in Latin America. Recent data (February 2012) from the Brazilian Federal Agency for Support and Evaluation of Postgraduate Education (CAPES)[15] show that the number of postgraduate programmes increased to 3,319 compared with 2,718 in 2010. In terms of courses (the same programme can have more than one course) Brazil had 2,871 Master's, 1,696 Doctorate and 393 Professional Master's. CAPES is responsible for awarding scholarship grants to postgraduate students at universities and research centres in Brazil and abroad, and whose central purpose is to coordinate efforts to improve the quality of Brazil's faculty and staff in higher education through grant programmes. At present CAPES supports about 22,000 students in Brazilian postgraduate programmes and 1,500 in other countries.

Enrolments in postgraduate programmes have increased to around 22% in the last 5 years, totalling more than 165,000 students distributed in around 2,800 programmes, 2,500 Master's degrees, 1,500 at doctorate level and almost 300 professional Master's, graduating over 12,000 Ph.D. students, 40,000 Master's and hundreds of professional Master's students each year. Brazil has more than 80,000 researchers and scholars engaged in research at private and governmental institutions. These achievements result from 60 years of systematic and continuous investment in higher education by the federal and state governments, including the creation of CAPES and the National Council for Scientific and Technological Development (CNPq)[16] (both established in 1951), and state agencies for research support, as in the State of São Paulo Research Foundation (FAPESP)[17]. CAPES, together with CNPq, other agencies and the private sector, are responsible for the programme (created by the Federal Government) *Science without Borders*[18], which aims to send 100,000 students and researchers abroad in the next 4 years, mostly concentrated in engineering and technological areas. The main objective of this programme is to enhance the internationalization level of Brazilian Science by offering scholarship grants on a large-scale basis for study abroad, expanding the involvement in science, technology, innovation and competitiveness, through the international mobility of students and researchers (Bertazzo, 2012).

The evaluation of the postgraduate programmes is conducted by CAPES, which uses an internationally recognized methodology; they increase continuously without losing academic quality, according to these frequent evaluations. This evaluation system serves as the basis for the formulation of public policies, mostly in planning budgets and support for the higher education system in Brazil. The postgraduate programmes are evaluated every 3 years, with scores ranging from 1 (lowest) to 7 (highest). Programmes with scores of 3 or below are closely monitored by CAPES and consistently re-evaluated when improvements have been made. If, after a well-defined period, the minima standards have not been reached, the programmes are closed.

Nevertheless, compared with the best international postgraduate programmes, Brazilian postgraduate studies generally tend to be more academic in nature, rather than professionally oriented; and more concentrated in the social sciences and humanities, with less emphasis on engineering and technology (Mota and Martins, 2008). Professional fields of study and career preparation are more commonly offered at the undergraduate level, and even at that level there is a clear asymmetry (i.e., a dominance of humanities in contrast with engineering and technological areas) compared with international standards. In addition, the emphasis on academic achievements in the assessments has acted as a stimulus to applied, technical and interdisciplinary programmes, especially those driven by demands from the non-academic sectors.

In the past decade the number of peer-reviewed papers from Brazil has increased dramatically from less than 1% of the world's total in 2000 to approximately 2.7% in 2010[19], making the country the thirteenth most successful publisher of papers in the world. Nevertheless, even with increased scientific activity, the number of patents has remained extremely low. Feder (2011) suggests that the Brazilian scientific community needs to shift its emphasis from quantity to quality and go beyond the production of scientific knowledge to move into the area of creating scientific products.

### 2.2.2 England and Wales

Our second national case study is England and Wales. Education in England and Wales is divided into primary, secondary, further and higher education sectors. Compulsory education lasts for 11 years, with statutory schooling ages between 5 to 16 years (Figure 2.2). In accordance with the UK Department of Education[20], during this time children are required to be in full-time education that is suited to their age, ability, aptitude and special educational needs. If a child does not attend school, the local education authority must be satisfied that other appropriate provision is available.

Most pupils transfer from primary to secondary school at the age of 11 years. Under the National Curriculum, as a result of the Education Reform Act 1988, four Key Stages to education have been established: Key Stage 1 (5 to 7 years old); Key Stage 2 (7 to 11 years old); Key Stage 3 (11 to 14 years old); and Key Stage 4 (14 to 16 years old). Pupils are assessed by National Curriculum tests at the end of each Key Stage. Key Stage 1 assessments are taken at age 7, Key Stage 2 assessments are taken at age 11 and Key Stage 3 assessments are taken at age 14. Key Stage 4 is assessed by levels of achievement acquired at General Certificate of Secondary Education (GCSE) level. Having completed GCSEs, pupils have a choice of whether to continue with further education at school or college or undertake employment.

In England and Wales there are several types of qualifications. General educational qualifications include GCSE, GCE A-level (General Certificate of Education Advanced Level) and AS (Advanced

*Figure 2.2 Teacher training and students at the Institute of Education, University of London in 1946.*

Supplementary) examinations. GCSEs are usually taken at the age of 15 to 16 in a wide range of subjects. Grades are issued on a scale from A* to G (A* being the highest grade). These are based on assessment throughout the course with an examination at the end of the course. GCE A-levels are assessed mainly by an examination at the end of the course and are usually taken by those who are 18 years or over. GCE AS-levels are of the same standard as GCE A-levels but cover less content. These were introduced to help pupils cover additional subjects, thus increasing the breadth of their education. Pupils aiming to pursue a higher educational level usually transfer to a higher education institution, college or university, at the age of 18 years. Many pupils continue with further education either at school or at further education institutions, which are increasingly offering a range of vocational courses, as well as academic courses.

General National Vocational Qualifications (GNVQs) are an alternative educational path for those entering further education at college or school. GNVQs combine general and vocational education with employment. They are based on the skills required by employers, combined with the development and understanding of skills needed in vocational areas. Vocational areas covered include business, health and social care or engineering. Specific to occupations are National Vocational Qualifications (NVQs) and these qualifications are based on skills, knowledge and competencies required by specific occupations set out by industry-defined standards. A number of standards are used to assess NVQs and these include observations within the workplace, oral questioning, practical and written questioning and assignments. A five-level framework is applied to NVQs, each level broadly equates to the following description: level 1, foundation skills in semi-skilled occupations; level 2, semi-skilled occupations; level 3, technician/skilled/craft/supervisory occupations; level 4, technician/junior management occupations; and level 5, professional/senior management occupations. The framework is divided into 11 areas of major sectors of industry and commerce and each area has various levels up to level 5. It is possible to progress into higher education or employment, having obtaining NVQs/SVQs (this last one is the Scottish version for the NVQs). Higher National Certificates (HNCs) and Higher National Diplomas (HNDs) are modular courses of vocational study mostly taken at college or school.

In the UK, Scotland, Northern Ireland, England and Wales all have very distinct educational systems, policies and curricula. As Harris and Gorard (2009:1) report, free elementary education was (near) universal in the UK by 1900. In order to achieve the same for secondary education, the government issued an Education Act in 1944 that made schooling mandatory up to the age of 15. Three types of schools prevailed in the following decades: *technical schools* which de-emphasized academic content and focused on the preparation of pupils for the crafts and trades; *grammar schools* which had the most academically oriented curriculum; and *secondary schools* which catered for the majority of children and offered a mixed academic, general and vocational curriculum. From the 1960s onward, most secondary institutions were converted into comprehensive schools.

Traditionally teachers had been granted autonomy in terms of the curriculum:

> ... there were no statutory guidelines as to which subjects should be covered, what materials should be dealt with in each subject, what was appropriate to a particular level, how one year's work led into another's, how learning should be planned and assessed, what feedback on progress should be made to parents and pupils.
>
> *(Coulby, 2000: 16)*

In 1992, all state schools were given financial autonomy under the control of the *Office for Standards in Education* (OFSTED). The first *National Curriculum* was a step towards greater control and homogenization of school subjects and the maintenance of particular teaching and learning standards controlled by a school inspection system (under the auspices of OFSTED), followed by the introduction of national league tables, labelling "good" and "poorly" performing schools (Harris and Gorard, 2009: 2). Core subjects of the National Curriculum include Mathematics, English and Science. Other foundation subjects at KS3 are Design and Technology, Information and Communication Technology, Geography, History, Music, Physical Education and Art. At KS4, in addition to the ones previously mentioned, Citizenship and a Modern Foreign Language (Harris and Gorard, 2009: 8) are studied. Further developments in the same direction were the *National Literacy Strategy* (1998) and the *National Numeracy Strategy* (1999), both of which established national curricular objectives and standards.

Since the election of the Labour Government in 1997, various reforms targeted issues like social exclusion, educational failure and access for all to quality education. This was meant to be achieved through increased regulation and governance of education, including the allocation of resources (depending on, for instance, the respective position of schools in league tables), the admission of pupils to schools and the appointment of staff, the formulation and control of contents and standards of teaching, and learning and assessment; for example, through the design of curricula and monitoring of its provision.

With regards to the last cornerstones in curricular reforms in England, the 14-19 Reform, Harris and Gorard (2009: 4) argue:

> In one sense these quite radical changes to the "national" curriculum for the late secondary phase are an admission of defeat. The social class stratification of educational participation and outcomes has outlasted the onset of universal secondary education, the raising of the school leaving age, the decline of grammar schools, the introduction of the National Curriculum, the establishment of (some) parental choice and national inspections, among other things.
> *(Harris and Gorard, 2009: 2)*

Education in England has gone through many changes in the last decades, among them, increased standardization, regulation and auditing of the education system.

While the social recognition of teachers had been continuously diminished, there is an increasing awareness that teachers are the essential element for improving educational systems. Therefore an increased emphasis is being placed on initial qualifications and the continuous professional development of teachers and principals, as indicated by the *Qualified Teacher Status* (QTS) and the *National Professional Qualification for Headship* (NPQH) qualifications. The focus on accountability and evaluation of performance has generally led to a marginalization of areas that are not, and can not, be assessed. Social class remains the key variable associated with educational participation and opportunity in the UK. There is considerable reproduction of status and education within families. In the next chapter we will focus on the idea of innovation and innovatory educational practices.

## NOTES

1. United Nations Educational, Scientific and Cultural Organization, UNESCO. Portal available at: http://www.unesco.org/new/en/. Accessed in December, 2012.
2. As seen in: http://www.unesco.org/education/tlsf/mods/theme_b/mod07.html. Accessed December, 2012.
3. The International Baccalaureate (IB) Foundation. Portal available at: http://www.ibo.org. Accessed August, 2012.
4. Brazilian Law 9394/1996, National Law establishing the Directives and Framework for the Education Sector, 1996.
5. National Council of Education, *Conselho Nacional de Educação*, CNE. Portal available at: http://portal.mec.gov.br/index.php?Itemid=754&id=12449&option=com_content&view=article. Accessed in July, 2012.
6. Brazilian Institute of Geography and Statistics, *Instituto Brasileiro de Geografia e Estatística*, IBGE. Portal available at: http://www.ibge.gov.br/english/. Accessed in August, 2012.
7. The new National Educational Plan (*Plano Nacional de Educação*, PNE) was sent by the Federal Government to the National Congress on December 15th, 2010, but it is still in discussion at the Brazilian Parliament.
8. Brazilian Education Development Plan, *Plano de Desenvolvimento da Educação*, PDE. Available at: http://portal.mec.gov.br/index.php?option=com_content&view=article&id=16478&Itemid=1107. Accessed in July, 2012.
9. Teacher's Portal, *Portal do Professor*. Portal available at: http://portaldoprofessor.mec.gov.br/index.html. Accessed in August, 2012.
10. Brazilian Open University, *Universidade Aberta do Brasil*, UAB. Portal available at: http://uab.capes.gov.br/. Accessed in August, 2012.
11. Brazilian Embassy. *Notes on the Brazilian Education System*. Academic Sector from Brazilian Embassy in London-UK, 2012.
12. National Institute of Studies and Educational Research Anísio Teixeira, INEP Portal. Available at: http://portal.inep.gov.br. Accessed April, 2012.

13. QS World University Rankings® has been published annually since 2004. QS World University Rankings® is one of the most trusted university rankings in the world. Available at: http://www.topuniversities.com/. Accessed August, 2012.

14. QS University Rankings: Latin America™. The same as Note 13 but for Latin America. Available at: http://www.topuniversities.com/university-rankings/latin-american-university-rankings/2012. Accessed August, 2012.

15. Brazilian Federal Agency for Support and Evaluation of Postgraduate Education, *Coordenação de Aperfeiçoamento de Pessoal de Nível Superior*, CAPES. Portal available at: http://www.capes.gov.br/. Accessed August, 2012.

16. National Council for Scientific and Technological Development, *Conselho Nacional de Desenvolvimento Científico e Tecnológico*, CNPq. Portal available at: http://www.cnpq.br/. Accessed August, 2012.

17. São Paulo Research Foundation, *Fundação de Amparo à Pesquisa do Estado de São Paulo*, FAPESP. Portal available at: http://www.fapesp.br/en/. Accessed August, 2012.

18. Science without Borders, *Ciência sem Fronteiras*. Available at: http://www.cienciasemfronteiras.gov.br/web/csf/. Accessed August, 2012.

19. As seen at: http://thomsonreuters.com/essential-science-indicators/. Accessed January, 2013.

20. UK Department of Education, as seen at: http://www.education.gov.uk/schools. Accessed October, 2012.

# CHAPTER 3

# Innovation

> *It ought to be remembered that there is nothing more difficult to take in hand, more perilous to conduct, or more uncertain in its success, than to take the lead in the introduction of a new order of things. Because the innovator has for enemies all those who have done well under the old conditions and lukewarm defenders in those who may do well under the new. This coolness arises partly from fear of the opponents, who have the laws on their side, and partly from the incredulity of men, who do not readily believe in new things until they have had a long experience of them.*
>
> **(Niccolò Machiavelli, 1953)**[1]

In general, innovation can be assumed to have occurred when knowledge is successfully introduced into, and valued by, organizations in such a way that it is formally organized, managed, realized and implemented in practice. In this chapter, we explore the concept of innovation and identify connections, relations and links between it *and* sustainability and knowledge-development. We suggest that the best way to connect economic development with sustainable social development is by adopting innovatory strategies. What this implies is a reworking of the traditional relationship between science, technology and innovation, so that rather than these three concepts being understood as linear in form and unidirectional, innovation now becomes more central, broader in concept and has the potentiality to feedback to the beginning of the knowledge creation process. We also review the various innovatory strategies adopted by Brazil and England.

## 3.1 THE CONCEPT OF INNOVATION

Innovation and innovatory practices are becoming more important in modern societies (Mota, 2009a, 2011). The concept and practice have changed over time; in the middle ages, the term was more often associated with novelty, arising from human creativity; whereas today it is more directly connected to the possibility of sustainable economic and social development. For example, Eugene Grasset (see Figure 3.1) suggests that innovation is central to our understanding of change processes, being both conserving and modifying.

*Figure 3.1 Work by Eugène Grasset/2012, translated from* Methode de Composition Ornamentale.

As the concept is now understood, it is much broader than simply technological innovation, although technology continues to be a significant driver of change, especially in the last two centuries. Godin (2008) understands innovation dialectically, so that events and happenings in the world give rise to new categories. These in turn contribute to, and allow material and social changes in the world, which again lead to new meanings being given to concepts such as innovation. During the Renaissance, artisans accepted that imitation was a beneficial practice, closely associated with the idea of novelty-innovation, and as being central to the notion of invention itself. For Newman (1989), this was art imitating nature, as the alchemists claimed. Imitation was considered at that time as requiring work, experimentation, judgement and imagination. By the beginning of the industrial revolution in England, imitation was associated with invention because it resulted in the production of new commodities, introducing not only the real possibility of meeting demand by diffusion and scale, but, in doing so, improving quality and design. As a result, innovation by imitation, although not primary, became associated with derivative or incremental innovation. The concept and the practice had moved on from mere copying.

Differences between discovery and invention have always been central to the meaning that a society gives to the idea of innovation. Discovery usually refers to a process of finding out things, whilst invention is more often associated with synthesizing, combining or making new things, such as objects, processes or new theories. During the eighteenth and nineteenth centuries, invention, initially associated with science, but also with imagination in literature and the visual arts, became increasingly identified with mechanical or technological invention (cf. Engell, 1981). However, during the twentieth century, with its emphasis on commodification, ownership and utilitarian valuing, technological innovation has become synonymous with invention, and also very often with innovation.

The term "innovation", although old (for instance, it is cited by Machiavelli in *The Prince* (1513) and by F. Bacon in *Of Innovations* (1625)[1]), was rarely used before the twentieth century. In contrast, in the last century there were a series of debates about innovation. Joseph Schumpeter wrote extensively about innovation in the first half of the last century, and he was probably the most influential thinker on innovation and the first economist to include the subject within a theory of economic development. Schumpeter (1961) argued that capitalism is a permanent *creative-destructive* system and innovation is the cause of this phenomenon. Innovation, he suggested, was essential for competitive survival. Nations, regions and enterprises are left behind when they are not as innovative as their competitors, resulting in increasing disparity in wealth between rich and poor countries. However, Schumpeter also argued that, while innovation was creative and beneficial, allowing for the rise of new industries, and generating wealth and jobs, it could also destroy established businesses and many products, and even produce higher unemployment.

Schumpeter (1961) identified five types of innovation. The first was the introduction of a new product, and the second was a new method of production. The third was the development of a new market. His fourth type of innovation referred to new sources of raw materials. Finally, he suggested that it might also result in new forms of organization. Schumpeter (1939: 128) distinguished between innovation and invention by arguing that: "innovation is possible without invention and invention does not necessarily induce innovation", only when commercialized. Innovation occurs in products, and new functionalities of previously existing products, services, and operational processes. These processes might include equipment and machinery, as products, and logistics in the form of providers' services. Innovation can be either radical or incremental. In general, it is radical when the nature of the product, service or process changes. However, most innovations are thought of as incremental when the improvements come from the application of new ideas to existing products and services, or even adjustments to organizational processes (Dodgson and Gann, 2010). Schumpeter also pointed to the inherent risks in innovatory practices, the argument being that an absence of risk and uncertainty would provide little advantage over competitors if everyone could innovate without them.

During the second half of the last century a number of authors (for example, Deutsch *et al.*, 1986; Mulgan *et al.*, 2007) introduced a broader understanding of innovation including that of *social innovation*, meaning either major advances in the social sciences, policy reforms for the betterment of society, or solutions to social problems. More recently, a new wave of innovatory approaches includes original concepts like *open innovation, democratizing innovation, creative economies*; and areas not usually thought of as being innovatory such as *organizational* and *marketing*. All of these relate to the idea that innovation, both etymologically and practically, is now multiply-sourced, and therefore does not just emerge from the traditional research laboratories and universities.

This constitutes a new and different form of knowledge-construction. Gibbons *et al.* (1994) characterized the new and old types of knowledge-development as two modes: *disciplinary forms of knowledge* normally produced by the academy and research laboratories, and *trans-disciplinary forms of knowledge* normally produced outside them. Mode One knowledge is linear, causal, cumulative, disciplinary, reductionist and has significant status in society. This has, they claim, been challenged by Mode Two forms of knowledge, where technology is understood as autonomous and able to develop outside of the academy, where it is trans-disciplinary, problem-solving, workplace-based, synoptic rather than reductionist, heterarchical and transient.

## 3.2 INNOVATION AND SUSTAINABILITY

Sustainability defines how human beings can satisfy their needs without compromising those of future generations. It has become a guiding principle for world economic development and is closely related to the way we educate our populations for such challenges. We are suggesting that the most effective way of connecting economic development with sustainable social development is to develop innovatory ways of living. The key to progress that is compatible with sustainability, particularly in times of economic crisis, is innovation associated with education. Sustainability has the potential to transform the competitive landscape, forcing companies and societies to change the way they think and act about products, technologies, processes, and business models.

The problem is the Janus (the Roman god of beginnings and transitions)-faced model of business and innovation currently operating in late capitalist economies. On the one hand, businesses and enterprises look towards maximizing profits, cheap labour markets, exploitation of the world's resources, high levels of production, and demand-led economies. On the other hand, the world's resources are finite, pollution levels are rising, inequalities within and between nations are growing, technological solutions are focused on the needs of the few at the expense of the many, and there is evidence that these forms of enterprise are causing irreparable damage to the environment. The key question therefore becomes: can we develop, in late capitalist societies, institutions that can combine innovation and innovatory practices *and* sustainability, and in particular, in relation to the preservation of the environment?

The dimensions of the problem can be better understood through a notion of the ecological footprint, which is defined as how much land and water a human population requires to produce the resources it consumes and to absorb its waste. It also tracks how much productive area, or bio-capacity, is available, in relation to how human activity has developed on our planet. About one quarter of the earth's surface, accounting for 11.3 billion hectares, can be considered as biologically productive, and thus as contributing to the regeneration of resources.

The global bio-capacity per inhabitant on earth can be found by dividing the biologically productive available area by 6.15 billion people. The result is 1.8 global hectares per capita. Previous studies (for example, Kitzes *et al.*, 2007; Seliger *et al.*, 2008) have identified humanity's total ecological footprint and the respective $CO_2$ portion of it from 1961 to 2001. Since 1985, resource consumption at the global level is higher than its ecological capacity. The global population has increased from 3.08 billion in 1961 to 6.15 billion in 2001. The total energy consumption in 2001 is more than seven times the amount in 1961. Today's world average bio-capacity per person of 1.8 hectares is no longer sufficient for all of the human activity on earth. Today, human beings use the equivalent of 1.5 planets to provide the resources we use and to absorb our waste. This means that it now takes the Earth one year and six months to regenerate what we use in a year. This metric allows us to calculate human pressure on the planet and illustrates the depth of the crisis currently facing the world. If everyone lived the lifestyle of the average citizen living in the United States of America, we would need five planets to sustain it.

The extent of the crisis is revealed more fully if the future development of poorer nations is considered in this scenario. If the ecological footprint values are compared with the United Nations Human Development Index (HDI)[2], it is possible to observe that most of the African and many Asian and Latin American countries present a favourable ecological footprint but at the same time have a low HDI (cf., Kitzes *et al.*, 2007; Seliger *et al.*, 2008). This has serious implications for developing innovatory business models and ways of understanding modern societies.

## 3.3 KNOWLEDGE-DEVELOPMENT

Knowledge-development is a contested activity and this is in part because research is framed by an epistemology of one type or another. There are four types of epistemic framework: *positivism/empiricism*, *interpretivism*, a *critical perspective*, and *postmodernism*. When the social sciences were beginning to develop in the nineteenth century, they did so under the shadow of the physical sciences. Therefore, as immature sciences they sought to mirror the procedures and approaches adopted by the natural sciences (or at least by a version of scientific methodology which rarely equated with how scientists actually behaved).

Such positivist/empiricist approaches can be characterized in the following way. There is a real world out there and a correct way of describing it. This allows us to think that doing research is simply a matter of following the right methods or procedures. It thus portrays research as mechanistic and algorithmic, and this allows us to forget that research is essentially a social practice. What also follows from this is that the knowledge produced from this algorithmic process is always considered to be superior to a common sense understanding of the world, by virtue of its systematicity and rigour. Science works by accumulating knowledge; that is, it builds incrementally on previous knowledge. However, it is hard to argue that the social sciences have developed a body of knowledge that presents unequivocal truths about its subject matter. We will address the reasons for this when we examine alternative perspectives and approaches, and in particular, the idea that theory always precedes observation. Twentieth- and twenty-first century philosophers have generally accepted that any observations we make about the world, including those that are central to the research process and can be construed as "facts", are always conditioned by prior understandings we have of the world. There are no theory-free facts, and this puts at risk the distinction made by positivists/empiricists between observation and theory.

The positivist/empiricist method equates legitimacy with science (although this is very much an idealized view of scientific activity) and is characterized as a set of general methodological rules. A clear distinction is made between knowers (or researchers) and people and objects in the world. Facts can be identified, free of the values and personal concerns of the observer. Thus, any assertions or statements we make about the world are about observable measurable phenomena. This implies that, if two researchers apply the correct method in the research process, they would come to the same conclusions. It is the correct application of the method that guarantees certainty and trust in the findings of a research project. Although these assumptions are significant in their own right, they give the impression that positivism and empiricism are simply highly idealized abstruse doctrines; however, research has important social consequences and speaks as an authority in the world about social and physical matters. In these terms, research can be judged in terms of three overarching criteria: its internal validity (whether experimentally the effects observed as a result of the intervention were actually caused by it and not by something else); its external validity (whether findings from the case being investigated could be generalized to other cases in time and place); and finally its objectivity (whether the preconceptions and biases of the researcher have been accounted for in the construction of the account and eliminated as influencing variables).

As we have suggested above, this view of research has been disputed by interpretivists, critical theorists and postmodernists, who in their turn have been criticized for not providing a way of doing research which fulfils the Enlightenment desire for universal knowledge that is shorn of superstition, personal preference and special pleading. Interpretivists, critical theorists and postmodernists thus sought to provide an alternative to a view of research which prioritized reduction to a set of variables, a separation between the knower and what they sought to know, a means for predicting and controlling the future, and a set of perfectly-integrated descriptions of the world, with a view of the social actor as mechanistic and determined. Interpretivist approaches provide one possible alternative. In interpretivism, researchers focus on the meanings that social actors construct about their lives and in relation to the world, and argue that human beings negotiate this meaning in their social practices. Human action cannot then be separated from meaning-making, and our experiences are organized through pre-formulated interpretive frames. We belong to traditions of thought, and the task of the researcher is to make sense of these interpretations, even though such interpretive activity is mediated by the researcher's own interpretive frames of reference. This is a practical matter for each individual, though of course they cannot make meanings on their own, as all meaning-making is located within culturally- and historically-located communities of practice. The field of study is therefore the meaningful actions of social actors and the social construction of reality; and one of the consequences is that the social sciences have to be treated as distinct from the natural sciences.

Understanding the world and our knowledge of it are therefore social and institutional practices, primed for investigation, but resistant to algorithmic and mechanistic methods used in the natural sciences. In these terms, research can be judged by four overarching criteria (cf., Lincoln and Guba, 2000). The work has to be credible; that is, it can be judged to be successful if it fairly represents the worldviews of the social actors who are the subject matter of the research. A second criterion is transferability, and the work is here judged to be successful if generalizations made from the original setting can be transferred to other settings and environments; that is, they are applicable. A third criterion is dependability where a judgement is made about the suitability of the methods, analytical approaches, writing procedures and styles in relation to the pre-determined intentions and purposes of the research programme. A fourth criterion is confirmability. This is where a judgement is made as to whether the inferences and interpretations used in the construction of the research text are the most sensible and efficacious, given the type of data, the purposes and intentions of the research programme, and the underlying frameworks adopted by the knowledge-maker or researcher.

Critical theorists and critical realists take the interpretivist critique of positivism/empiricism one stage further. In the search for a disinterested universal knowledge, they look for a solution either in communicative competence (critical theorists) or in the structured nature of reality itself (critical realists). We will focus here on the former and in particular Habermas' (1987) argument that any claim to validity in research must be able to make the following assertions: (i) this work is intelligible and hence meaningful in the light of the structuring principles of the discourse community it is positioned within; (ii) what is being asserted propositionally is true; (iii) what is being explained can be justified; and (iv) the person who is making these claims is sincere about what they are asserting. These four conditions, if they are fulfilled, allow a researcher to say something meaningful about reality. The aim above all for a critical theorist is to develop knowledge that is potentially transformative or emancipatory: to detect and unmask those practices in the world which limit human freedom. Its purposes are, therefore, the direct replacement of one set of values (unjust, muddled and discriminatory) with another (rational, just and emancipatory).

The fourth framework is a postmodernist one, and again it should be noted that it was developed in reaction to positivist and empiricist frameworks for research and to all those epistemologies that posit a real world separate from the activities of the knower. As Lather (1991) suggests, any work or piece of research should give a voice to those social actors who have been traditionally marginalized (an explicit emancipatory purpose) and, in the process, (i) undermine and subvert the agendas held by those with more power in the world than others; (ii) surface for public discussion those textual devices (both spoken and written) used in conventional research; (iii) suggest ways of countering these powerful research constructions; (iv) question how researchers construct their texts and organize their sets of meaning in the world; and (v) re-introduce the researcher into the research text by locating them within those frameworks that act to construct them as researchers and as human beings.

All these research frameworks cannot be equally correct and this explains why researchers produce conflicting and contradictory results about important educational and social matters. However, the situation is more serious than this, since even though researchers may subscribe to the same epistemology, they may still disagree with one another, even if they are focusing on the same set of social problems. The dispute might be about the correct and incorrect uses of the method, different views and interpretations of the epistemological tradition to which they claim to belong, or using different interpretive frameworks in relation to the data-set which has been collected. Frequently, qualitative and quantitative researchers disagree about a view of reality, even when they both operate from the same perspective. This has been called "the crisis of representation", and it is hard to imagine how one can escape from it, as the alternative is to revert back to a pre-Enlightenment time of knowledge being privileged by those who could command the most attention.

However, research is too important to simply ignore the problems of representation that we have alluded to above. Indeed, we need to understand how research texts are constructed and how power is ever present in their construction. This is because research is conducted with and through other people (some of them more powerful than others), and the researcher is always in the business of collecting accounts by social actors of their lifeworlds and activities in the world. These accounts are always self-serving. What we mean by this is not that they are wrong *per se*, but that they are living documents, which enable the respondent to go on in life. They are thus always conditional and this works in four ways: (i) social actors are unaware of some of the conditions for their actions (every action has a set of conditions underpinning it—for example, a speech act requires a language, vocabulary and grammar); (ii) they are unlikely to be able to predict all the consequences of their actions, so there are going to be unintended consequences; (iii) social actors may not be aware of much of their own knowledge and expertise—in other words, much of their knowledge is tacit, and thus they cannot, except with the greatest of difficulty, bring it to the surface in their accounts of their lives; and (iv) equally they may be motivated by unconscious forces and impulsions which they find great difficulty in articulating.

What we can say then about knowledge-making is this. However it is conceived, it has an authority about it which distinguishes it from opinion, superstition, conjecture, rhetoric, speculation or supposition. It has a connection with an external reality, though this is never straight-forward, since language rarely acts in an unmediated way in research. Knowledge-making of whatever persuasion is underpinned by a set of beliefs focusing on: (i) how the words, propositions and texts relate to an external reality; (ii) how the researcher is immersed in the process of knowledge construction (this means that the ideal of a disinterested, dispassionate and impartial researcher is a convenient fiction which bears little relation to the reality of doing research); (iii) what the underpinning purposes of the research are (is it descriptive, theoretical, transformative or transgressive?); and finally, (iv) how such research can be judged (whether it is: validated by respondents from the research setting, and this goes beyond affirmation of the truthfulness of events or activities; grounded in the data; transformative of the setting it is focusing on; consistent and coherent; relevant in some specified way; or it surfaces underlying power relations in the research setting and as a consequence repositions players in the game).

## 3.4 KNOWLEDGE-DEVELOPMENT AND INNOVATION

We suggested above that the social sciences emerged under the shadow of the physical sciences and to some extent the methods, epistemologies and strategies they employed mirrored those of the established physical sciences. Indeed, the Enlightenment in Europe heralded a new scientific revolution, which has influenced all the different types of knowledge-development in the modern era. We also suggested that knowledge-development in the social sciences took a number of different forms, resulting in phenomenological, critical and post-modernist epistemic revolutions. One of these new epistemic forms was an intensely practical one, that of knowledge-development through the Research and Development (R&D) sector. Research and Development activities range from very practical and quick problem-solving to basic research, essentially driven by curiosity and with less concern as to its immediate application.

In 1963, the Organization for Economic Cooperation and Development (OECD) in Frascati, Italy, published a manual[3] for policy-makers describing and proposing a standard practice for surveys of research and development. In the Frascati Manual, R&D is described as having three elements: (i) basic research in experimental or theoretical work undertaken primarily to acquire new knowledge of the underlying foundation of phenomena and observable facts, without any particular application or use in mind; (ii) applied research is also considered to be original investigation undertaken in order to acquire new knowledge (however, it is directed primarily towards a specific practical aim or objective); and (iii) experimental development is systematic work, drawing on existing data gathered from research and/or practical experience, where the aim is to produce new processes, systems, and services, or to improve substantially those already produced or installed.

Basic and applied forms of research are points on a continuum, with many interconnections. A generalized linear model was produced in the twentieth century, which suggested that innovation starts with basic research. It then becomes applied research, is developed as a product, and finally, is used by people in society. The last two steps are more associated with innovation. What we can observe today is that innovation is no longer a distant consequence of basic research. Innovation becomes in many instances the origin of the research programme and, as a consequence, moderates and stimulates the science itself. At the same time, the traditional assumption that innovation results from meeting demand is replaced by the idea that sometimes innovation also generates demand which previously had never been imagined. This suggests a simplified knowledge management scheme (see Figure 3.2).

Starting from basic data, through its synthesis and organization, systematic information is generated. This in part promotes education and skills development, allowing for general knowledge to be transferred from generation to generation. The specific fraction of general knowledge, which is based on the scientific method, is recognized as modern science, which is closely associated with technology and innovation.

```
Modern Science – Technology and Innovation
        ↑  (Scientific Method)
      General Knowledge
        ↑  (Education and skill-development)
      Systematic Information
        ↑  (Synthesis)
      Basic Data (raw).
```

*Figure 3.2 Knowledge-development management scheme.*

```
Science  →  Technology  →  Innovation
            (Time-Sequenced)
```

*Figure 3.3 Science-Technology-Innovation time-sequence traditional model.*

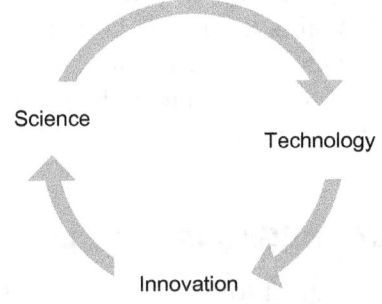

*Figure 3.4 Science-Technology-Innovation model, time-sequenced in accordance with a contemporary circular relationship.*

With regards to science, traditionally, the model in Figure 3.3 was considered to be the norm. However, a new model (see Figure 3.4) now has more credence.

Innovation is becoming more central in the knowledge-development process, broader in scope and it is both an end-product and a stimulant for knowledge in its own right.

Suh (2010) argues that there are three necessary conditions for the occurrence of innovatory practices. The first of these is that all steps or elements of an innovation continuum are present. The second is that an innovation hub can be nucleated if the initial size of the nucleate is larger than a critical size and if the activation energy barrier for nucleation can be overcome. Finally, the last requires that the nucleation rate must be faster than the rate at which innovative talents and ideas can diffuse away from the region. In this new scenario, educational institutions have increasingly played a central role in science, technology and innovation-based economic development, and the role of universities and research centres has evolved from performing conventional research and educational functions to serving as innovation-promoting knowledge hubs.

The traditional university, in general, looks backwards and understands itself as a storehouse or accumulator of old knowledge. On the other hand, the modern university sees itself as a generator of technological innovation and economic development in its region (Youtiea and Shapira, 2008). Where innovation is the central issue, universities are simultaneously central generators, essentially motivated by external demands, and repositories of knowledge. The way that knowledge is developed, disseminated and applied affects not only the cultural richness of the society, but also its global competitiveness. To meet the challenges of competitiveness, appropriate policies are necessary to encourage and facilitate closer understanding and joint work between universities and the productive sector.

## 3.5 INNOVATION STRATEGIES IN BRAZIL

The presence of *start-ups* through the enterprise incubators inside Brazilian universities contributes to the integration of undergraduate and postgraduate programmes. Student participation in enterprise simulations are becoming an integral part of the curriculum, as is the use of case studies, and the solving of practical and real-life problems for Master's and Doctorate theses. Traditionally, in Brazil, education and the productive sector have been clearly differentiated. Evidence of this differentiation in Brazil can be seen, for instance, in the 2012 annual World Competitiveness Yearbook (WCY)[4], recently published by the International Institute for Management Development (the IMD Business School), reflecting how countries manage their economic and human resources to increase their prosperity. In accordance with them, the most competitive of the 59 ranked economies in 2012 are Hong Kong, the United States and Switzerland, with the United Kingdom occupying eighteenth position. Emerging economies, like Brazil (ranked 48th), China (23rd), India (35th) and Russia (46th) are not yet immune to the international turmoil.

In Brazil, in order to confront the lack of entrepreneurial spirit, funding agencies, mostly associated with innovation promotion, were created, such as the Federal Government Financing Agency for Projects and Studies (FINEP)[5], with greater emphasis on technology and knowledge transfer to industry. The financial relationship between the programmes and the local industries was, and to some extent remains, minimal compared to other countries with similar academic systems. For a long time, Brazilian and international companies located in Brazil concentrated on short-term profits, based on imported technologies and dependent on the financial markets. Long-term investments were considered to be unproductive. However, these trends are rapidly changing. Economic globalization and the new role played by the country internationally are contributing to Brazilian industries facing tougher competition and, with inflation now under control, they can no longer depend on profits from capital markets, as in the past.

There is some evidence that universities are now playing an important and necessary role in the country's entrepreneurial and innovation ecosphere. University-based incubator programmes are flourishing. According to the World Bank's sponsored *Infodev*[6] partnership of aid agencies, 75% of companies supported by incubators are still operating three years later. In accordance with the National Association for Promotion of Innovation and Entrepreneurship, ANPROTEC[7], Brazil's incubator network has developed from 136 in 2000 to over 500 today (cf., Mota, 2013). The country leads one of the most successful incubation movements in Latin America, with incubator models that are bottom-up, service-oriented, suited to regional needs, and having universities as their facilitators. The new regulatory legal framework, including the Federal Innovation Law (2004) and the Good Will Law (2005), has also contributed to building other programmes over the past 6 years that focus on technological innovation. An example of this includes the government's efforts to recognize the importance of universities in the entrepreneurial ecosystem by passing a law that grants university professors and academic researchers temporary leave to create *start-ups* or provide tax exemptions for innovatory enterprises.

With regards to the difficulties of starting new enterprises in Brazil, there is space for improvement in the policy realm. Brazil's *Ease of Doing Business* rank in the World Bank's Doing Business project is 129 out of 183 economies (cf., Mota, 2013). Starting a business in Brazil takes 120 days; double the average for Latin American and Caribbean countries and far longer than the average 13 days for OECD[8] countries. Brazilian entrepreneurs also face a complex tax system and difficulties in accessing finance. Moreover, entrepreneurship education is falling behind, according to Endeavor Brazil[9]; less than 10% of Brazilians aged 18–64 receive any type of entrepreneurship education.

Throughout the country, entrepreneurs are exploring market-based solutions to poverty-related problems, including access to quality education, affordable housing, health care services, and information technology. Brazilian entrepreneurs are seeking to address the needs of this marginalized population; entrepreneurs in Brazil have a vast market of up to 200 million people with growing purchasing power. The middle class is expanding with more than 30 million people moving from class D and class E since 2003. The projection for the richer classes (A and B) is that in 2 years they will have increased by more than 30 million people, making the country a land of opportunity.

The Brazilian economy is increasingly focusing on the production, transmission and consumption of information and technology. It would therefore be expected that the education sector would keep abreast of these economic trends. However, there is some evidence to suggest that, although the Brazilian economy is modern and highly competitive, the education system, at primary, secondary and tertiary levels, has not kept apace. Over the past 10 years, the Brazilian economy has averaged 3.2% annual GDP growth; in 2010 the country had an impressive 7.5% growth rate. The Brazilian economy, led by the agricultural, manufacturing and mining sectors, is booming. As a direct consequence of this economic growth, from 2001 to 2009 poverty rates dropped from 35% to 21% of the total population, although this still leaves more than 40 million Brazilians living below the poverty line, statistics established by the World Bank.

During 2012 the overvalued currency had weakened from its peak of 1.54 *Reias* in July 2011 to 2.0 *Reais* to the US Dollar. After the Federal Government's decision to cut returns on government-backed savings accounts, the Central Bank's policy interest rate at around 8% is near to an historic low and is likely to fall even further. These facts are welcomed by manufacturers, who had been operating with an inflated currency rate and high interest rates for years. Brazil's terms of trade improved by around 25% between 2000 and 2010 and, in the past 5 years, private-sector credit doubled; but even then, investment is only around 19% of GDP. In summary, in terms of market arrangements, Brazil is becoming a major player in a world that is becoming more competitive. To survive and do well, any contemporary country needs to develop the levels of skills of its workforce and the qualities of the products and services it provides.

Topping the list of economic areas for development is agriculture and the processing of foodstuffs. These account for about a quarter of Brazil's GDP and 36% of its exports. This is an area where a very successful technology transfer occurred from academia, especially from the federal Brazilian agency, EMBRAPA[10], to the productive sector. Over the last 20 years, Brazil has become the world's largest producer of sugarcane, coffee, and tropical fruits. It has the world's largest commercial cattle herd (50% larger than that of the US) at 170 million animals. Also, oil is expected to become the next big commodity for export, especially if a way can be found to drill safely in the Atlantic Ocean's deep waters. Reserves are believed to equal those shared by Norway and the UK in the North Sea. The promotion of innovation and appropriate professional training are becoming key strategies for sustainable development in the new economic settlement in Brazil, although connections between education and innovation are still undeveloped in the policy sphere. This success story is not mirrored in the economic decline of the United Kingdom.

## 3.6 INNOVATION STRATEGIES IN ENGLAND

The Technology Strategy Board[11] was established as a separate organization in 2007. It is a non-departmental public body sponsored by the Department for Business, Innovation and Skills. The Technology Strategy Board's main target is to make the United Kingdom a global leader in innovation by acting as a magnet for innovative businesses.

This is achieved by helping locally-produced state-of-the-art technology to be applied quickly, effectively and sustainably, and creating the appropriate environment to generate wealth and enhance the quality of life. In the Autumn of 2010, the British Government published the Technology Strategy Board's first strategic plan, launched in 2008, and also confirmed the Board as the United Kingdom's innovation agency, with the role of being the primary public body in the United Kingdom for business innovation. Although in a different economic and political environment, the consequences of the financial crisis of 2008 are still present and the need for innovation is even greater than before. It means that, for the British Government, growth is a central priority and innovation a key enabler for business competition.

*Connect and catalyse* was the title of the first plan and it is still the main driving principle for promoting opportunities to connect partners and networks and enable businesses to transform ideas into the products and services of tomorrow[12]. The United Kingdom intends to compete effectively and in a sustainable way in the globalization process, which, at the same time, brings opportunities and challenges. Meeting these challenges will depend on rapid technological innovation, as well as effective strategic management of knowledge. It is clear that the United Kingdom's investments in innovation have tended to be later and lower than is desirable for sustainable growth. From 2008 to 2011, the agency delivered over £2 billion of innovation in a wide range of areas. Challenge-led programmes such as innovation platforms were introduced, which attempted to create communities that would stimulate sustainable UK business growth. In particular, a Small Business Research Initiative (SBRI)[13] was launched to promote innovation in that specific sector.

For the future, five main areas have been chosen as the strategic focus: (i) accelerating the journey between concept and commercialization, which is often fragmented and hard for businesses to accomplish; (ii) connecting the different elements of the innovation landscape, and helping to define European Union (EU) funding programmes, while enabling businesses to benefit from EU and international opportunities; (iii) turning government action into business opportunities, modifying traditional markets and creating new opportunities for innovative businesses; (iv) investing in priority areas based on potential, and establishing themes most likely to generate sustainable United Kingdom economic growth; and (v) continuously improving capability, supporting and developing existing talent and ensuring a positive and stimulating environment to work collaboratively.

The innovation plan includes key commitments such as: (i) technology and innovation centres, which are physical centres of excellence appropriate to helping businesses to develop and commercialize good projects; (ii) new support for high potential small and medium-sized enterprises (SMEs), which should be the major source of the United Kingdom's future economic growth; (iii) public procurement, at about £220 billion per year, providing opportunities for governments acting as "intelligent lead customers", making the public sector procurement a force for innovation; (iv) large-scale demonstrator projects contributing to overcome barriers, stimulating partners to make possible new products closer to the market; and (v) new forms of knowledge exchange, where online social networks can constitute efficient connectors, allowing bridging mechanisms for entrepreneurs with projects and resources.

Recently, Britain's economic performance has received surprisingly good news from the Switzerland-based World Economic Forum (WEF)[14], which suggests that the United Kingdom is now the eighth-most competitive country in the world. Nevertheless, the same WEF points out that the United Kingdom's macroeconomic environment, the general health of the economy, remains weak, with the country ranked 110th in the world, down from 85th in 2011[15]. In line with the Global Competitiveness WEF Index[16], among 144 analysed countries, the leader is Switzerland, followed by Singapore, Finland, Sweden, Netherlands, Germany, United States and the United Kingdom. Brazil remains in the same 48th position as in the previous Index (2011–2012). Sir John Parker, chairman of mining group Anglo American, argued recently[17] that the foundations of Britain's industrial base, especially innovation, should be protected from severe spending cuts, since the chancellor has warned that the British Government may have to prolong austerity measures until 2018.

There is a proposition coming from the business sector, which still has to be discussed and approved by the policy-makers and legislators. This proposition suggests that all government procurement contracts, from train-building to school construction, should include a levy that will go to a central innovation fund for research in the industrial and manufacturing sectors. At the same time, the Royal Academy of Engineering, aiming to promote excellence in engineering, has created an enterprise hub that makes its members available to give advice on turning research into industrial products. In the next chapter we will address the issue of educating for innovatory practices.

## NOTES

1. The book "The Prince" is a political treatise written by Niccolo Machiavelli in 1513 and the book "Of Innovations" is an essay by Francis Bacon written in 1625.
2. From "Global Footprint Network. Advancing in Science and Sustainability". Available at: http://www.footprintnetwork.org/en/index.php/GFN/. Accessed August, 2012.
3. About the Frascati Manual: Proposed Standard Practice for Surveys on Research and Experimental Development, 6th edition, see: http://www.oecd.org/innovation/innovationinsciencetechnologyandindustry/frascatimanualproposedstandardpracticeforsurveysonresearch-andexperimentaldevelopment6thedition.htm. Accessed December, 2012.
4. From the 2012 World Competitiveness Yearbook (WCY), announced by IMD Business School. Available at: http://www.imd.org/news/IMD-announces-its-2012-World-Competitiveness-Rankings.cfm. Accessed July, 2012.
5. Federal Government Financing Agency for Projects & Studies, Brazilian agency *Financiadora de Estudos e Projetos,* FINEP. See more at: http://www.finep.gov.br/. Accessed December, 2012.
6. From INFODEV Portal. Available at: http://www.infodev.org. Accessed April, 2012.
7. Brazilian Association for Promotion of Innovation and Entrepreneurship, *Associação Nacional de Entidades Promotoras de Empreendimentos Inovadores*, ANPROTEC, see more at: http://www.anprotec.org.br/. Accessed July, 2012.
8. The Organization for Economic Co-operation and Development (OECD). See more at: http://www.oecd.org/about/. Accessed July, 2012.
9. Endeavor Brazil. See more at: http://www.endeavor.org.br/. Accessed July, 2012.
10. Brazilian Agriculture Research Corporation, *Empresa Brasileira de Pesquisa Agropecuária*, EMBRAPA, see more at: http://www.embrapa.br/english. Accessed August 2012.
11. The Technology Strategy Board. See more at: http://www.innovateuk.org/. Accessed September 2012.
12. The details of the agency's approach to accelerate the pace of innovation over the coming period is captured in the new strategy document, *Concept to Commercialisation*, published in May 2011 and accessible at the website cited in Note 11.
13. To see more about Small Business Research Initiative (SBRI) go to: http://www.innovateuk.org/deliveringinnovation/smallbusinessresearchinitiative.ashx. Accessed May, 2012.
14. World Economic Forum, WEC. See more at: http://www.weforum.org/reports/global-competitiveness-report-2011-2012. Accessed June, 2012.
15. The latest official statistics, as seen in: http://www.guardian.co.uk/business/2012/aug/24/uk-gdp-revised-economy-double-dip. Accessed August, 2012.
16. The Global Competitiveness WEF Index, as seen at: http://www3.weforum.org/docs/WEF_GlobalCompetitivenessReport_2012-13.pdf. Accessed June, 2012.
17. As seen at: http://www.guardian.co.uk/politics/2012/nov/18/cut-health-and-education-john-parker. Accessed December, 2012.

# CHAPTER 4

# The Third Educational Revolution

*In writing the history of the early reading brain, I was surprised to realize that questions raised more than two millennia ago by Socrates about literacy address many concerns of the early twenty-first century. I came to see that Socrates' worries about the transition from an oral culture to a literate one and the risks it posed, especially for young people, mirrored my own concerns about the immersion of our children into the digital world. Like the ancient Greeks we are embarked on a powerfully important transition—in our case from a written culture to one that is more digital and visual.*

**(Maryanne Wolf, 2007)**

As a result of the increased importance given to innovation in contemporary society and the availability of new educational technologies, we are entering the third educational revolution. This would suggest new ways of teaching and learning, as well as new approaches to knowledge production and transfer. Traditional teaching and learning approaches associated with the first and second educational revolutions (the building of the school and the invention of the printing press resulting in the modern printed book) are rapidly becoming redundant, as the digital revolution becomes entrenched. This would suggest that traditional approaches to learning (i.e., observation, coaching, goal clarity, mentoring, peer learning, simulation, instruction, concept-formation, reflection, meta-cognitive learning, problem-solving and practice) need to be developed as new digital technologies, and that, as a consequence, learning should be reconfigured as parts of the life course.

If we put to one side the issue of time flows (i.e., linear, stepped, recursive) we can identify the life course in different ways. Firstly, this life course is understood as a *stepped system of statuses*. The learner moves from a lower status to a higher status—a series of status steps—where status is understood as the accord given to the position attained by the person. A learning transition is understood as movement between these steps. Secondly, the life course is seen as a *stepped system of learning markers*. This can be either formal or informal. The first is in formal terms, an example might be sectorial (e.g., pre-school to primary to secondary to post-compulsory, etc.). The second is in terms of informal conceptually-orientated learning stages; for example, Jean Piaget's (1952) schema comprising progression from concrete operational to formal operational thinking, or Lawrence Kohlberg's (1981) stages of moral thought, where the subject progresses from pre-moral and conventional rule conformity levels to the acceptance of general rights and standards, and even to adopting individual principles of conduct. A learning transition is then understood as movement between these stages.

Thirdly, the life course can be understood as a *stepped system of resource accumulations*. Resources are here defined as capital accumulations, such as cultural, social, economic and emotional. A transition is understood as movement in one direction between the different accumulation episodes. Fourthly, the life course is conceived of as a *stepped system of learning events*, and thus it is age-related. Here the formal system is given priority. This is the traditional form given to the life course, and it refers to learning events such as: birth, school, marriage, motherhood, death, etc. Movement then is understood as progression through these life-determining moments. And finally, the life course can be seen as a *stepped system of identity moments*. This is the most controversial because it involves the identification of a stable system of identity; or in this case a series of stable identities, and the person moves between them. Some examples are induction, self-realization, progression in learning, etc. The learning transition is from one identity moment to another.

Within the life course, the nature and constitution of learning is changing rapidly. It is now understood as an activity which is life-long and of a long duration, rather than a formal activity that takes place in designated institutions of teaching and learning at set points (and usually early) in the life course. Furthermore, the scope of learning has been extended, so that instead of referring just to the acquisition of knowledge, it now focuses on knowledge, skills and dispositions, such as interdisciplinary collaborations, working as a team, establishing networks, and problem solving abilities. What this requires is the development of new pedagogic approaches, new models of teaching and learning, a new understanding of how learning fits into the life course and a new accommodation with technologies. Both of these are directly related to educational processes and other technologies that have only a tangential relation with education.

Table 4.1 (see over page) schematically shows the three principal educational revolutions, and in particular how technology has impacted on educational processes. These educational revolutions do not replace each other overnight and there is not a clean break between them; however, what this schema does show are three distinct periods of educational change, driven by technological innovation. We are just at the beginning of the third educational revolution.

These three educational revolutions are driven by new educational technologies: in the first place, the invention of the school; in the second place, the creation of the printed book; and in the third place, the introduction of digital technologies.

## 4.1 THE SCHOOL

In Ancient Greece, Athens, during the fifth and fourth century BC, anyone could start up a school, decide on its curriculum, charge a fee, and recruit students, usually boys, although some girls were admitted. The curriculum focused on gymnastics, music and literacy, and was designed for children between the ages of 7 and 14. Those who could afford to continue their education after the age of 14 studied with the sophists: travelling teachers whose responsibility was to train and educate the sons of Athenian citizens, and from whom they could learn additional subjects such as rhetoric, mathematics, geography, natural history, politics and logic (Cordasco, 1976). Rafaello Sanzio's painting in Figure 4.1 is an example of one such sophist school.

These schools were very different from modern schools, and the classes were basically composed of rhetoric and oratory. Instructors or teachers were peripatetic and the mode of learning was principally didactic and text-based. Socrates was not a sophist himself, although people would ask him for advice on matters of practical conduct and solving educational problems. Socrates was a philosopher and a lover of wisdom, and introduced a new approach to learning, the so-called "Socratic method". It is a form of enquiry and debate in which the two opposing disputants argue from different positions by challenging the foundations of each other's argument. It is a negative method of hypothesis elimination, as better theories—identifying and then discarding those ideas that are progressively shown to be inadequate, illogical or contradictory—are developed. Plato, Socrates' best

Table 4.1 Three Educational Revolutions and their Principal Characteristics

| Period | Time | Place | Symbol | Characteristic | Audience | Purpose | Method |
|---|---|---|---|---|---|---|---|
| First Educational Revolution | V–IV BC | Ancient Greece | School | Able to learn from teachers' manuscripts; teacher dependent | Low accessibility | Knowledge to knowledge; teaching to think | Didactic and text-based |
| Second Educational Revolution | XV AD | Europe | Book | Independent learning, separately from the teacher | Potentially high accessibility, but restricted by low levels of literacy | Knowledge to technology; functional learning | Interpretation of the text and non-reliance on teacher interpretation |
| Third Educational Revolution | XXI AD | Global | Digital technologies | Flexible learning environments | High accessibility with high levels of literacy | Knowledge to technology; education for innovation | Independent learning; flexibility of learning setting |

*Figure 4.1 Fresco by Rafaello Sanzio/151: The School of Athens.*

student, was the principal person responsible (together with his own students) for writing down his master's ideas.

In 387 BC, Plato established a school in Athens, "the Academy", based on a different ethic and philosophy, which survived for the next nine centuries and can be seen as the foundation for the kind of school we know today. Founded for the education of youth, it was originally planned to educate disciples and philosophers, who would go on to occupy positions of authority in the state and be guided by true philosophy. If it is correct to say that most of Plato's books were built on the wisdom of Socrates, it is also correct to say that Plato took his own thoughts to a very high level, arguing that reality was known only through the mind, independent of the world of the senses (cf., Mota et al., 2003). Plato's Academy was different from most institutions of its time, because it was organized as a complex and diverse community, rather than as a simple teaching and learning arrangement between a master and his pupils (cf., Lynch, 1972: 75). In addition to being a formal school, it was also a place to meet people who were interested in studying mathematics, philosophy, and astronomy. In this sense, Plato's Academy was the world's first university and constituted the hearthstone of the Platonic tradition in philosophy (Pedersen, 1997).

If Plato was Socrates' best student, Plato's best student in turn was Aristotle, whose father was the personal physician to King Philip II of Macedon, Alexander the Great's father. At the age of eighteen, Aristotle went to Athens and became a student at the Academy. When Aristotle arrived in Athens to study at the Academy, it had already been open for 20 years. He spent 20 more years as a student and also as a teacher at the Academy. There, mathematics and science were taught, as well as philosophical dialect. In 347 BC, Aristotle left Athens, partly because he had disagreements with teachers at the Academy and when he returned in 335 BC, he founded "the Lyceum", a peripatetic school. Although influenced by Plato, Aristotle developed his own philosophy. In addition, he theorized and wrote about astronomy, physics, zoology, ethics, politics, aesthetics, music, drama, tragedy and poetry. He disagreed with Plato about many matters, including his suggestion that human beings are born with previous knowledge, but instead argued that knowledge comes from experience. He was thus the precursor of the revolution in philosophy which came to be known as empiricism, or, in one of its versions, logical empiricism.

Aristotle's new school, with a large library, was very successful and able to compete with the Academy, despite the fact that the philosophy taught there, at least initially, was based on Plato's work. Aristotle based his ideas of teaching on his education, and as he was himself a member of the Academy, it is only to be expected that the school he founded in the Lyceum would bear, at least at the beginning, a resemblance to Plato's school. Later, and gradually, Aristotle's school developed a new philosophy, and a new way of teaching. Like the Academy, the Lyceum was a very public place and the scholars used to spend long periods of time discussing and researching in an informal setting. The students were not made to attend school, and if one needed to work while attending the school, that was allowed. The teachers were encouraged to be intellectually independent from the scholars and to spread the Greek education system throughout the world (cf., Lynch, 1972).

Another interesting difference between the two schools was that Plato sought to educate by teaching, while Aristotle wished to educate through experiential research (Pedersen, 1997). In doing this, he introduced many new qualities into the Lyceum that the Academy did not have. One important quality was that Aristotle used a collection of previous literature and created a systematic amassing of information and material, generally in order to develop a whole field of knowledge. As a consequence, scholars were able to use previous collections of work to teach accurate information and then draw new conclusions, rather than using information which had remained broadly similar for decades (Lynch, 1972).

Aristotle also created a closer relationship between the head of the school and his fellow-scholars, and viewed higher education differently from most philosophers of that time, which affected the way he ran his school. This is one of the reasons why Plato's Academy is significantly different from Aristotle's Peripatetic School. In addition, Plato, at the Academy, used a dialectical method, which is a method of argument for solving disagreement where each participant uses logical reasoning to support their argument and eventually a conclusion is formed. In contrast, Aristotle recommended to his students that they should go out into the world and collect information, classify it, and synthesize it, seeking further information from people such as hunters and fishermen who had experience in the natural world. Aristotle's disagreement with the dialectical method led him to a belief in discussing less and instructing more. However, as Aristotle moved away from the Socratic or dialectical method, he began to experiment with visual and multimodal forms of expression, because he argued that learners learn best when different symbolic systems are used in conjunction; for example, words, images, diagrams and illustrations. This has had a significant influence on pedagogic methods since Aristotle first used it.

Plato and Aristotle had different ideas on public expositions. Plato did not believe that public shows should form a significant element of the educative process, whereas Aristotle gave instruction to his students in the evenings in an open forum while also lecturing publicly in the mornings. While Plato believed that teaching scholars meant only teaching those scholars who attended his Academy, Aristotle taught anyone and everyone who wanted to learn. One of his main goals was to share his knowledge, and spread that knowledge as far as possible (Lynch, 1972). In part, this difference can be explained by the respective status and position of the two men; Aristotle had a less secure position in the city of Athens than Plato did. Aristotle was not an Athenian citizen, and his connections with Macedonia (Aristotle tutored Alexander the Great and Alexander was the Greek King of Macedon) made the Lyceum appear as a pro-Macedonian school.

We are suggesting here that the most significant characteristic of the first educational revolution was the development of what we might call a school, a place of learning, even if early manifestations were developmental and dependent on the drive and charisma of key teachers, such as Plato and Aristotle. Because they had very different philosophies, and these translated into very different forms of pedagogy, the types of learning in their respective schools had more differences than similarities. However, subsequent schooling developed out of these initial attempts at formalizing the educative process.

## 4.2 THE BOOK

During the Ancient Greek period in Athens, although Socrates was inclined to minimize the importance of the written word, it was becoming more and more widespread through the common use of the Greek alphabet. Writing had existed for thousands of years, but it had, until recently, been the exclusive domain of scribes, government administrators, and religious elites. The common adoption of the Greek alphabet, as well as the Phoenician and Aramaic alphabets, made it possible for a wider group of people to learn to write. This in turn contributed to the emergence of a class of educated artisans and merchants who relied on the written word, and needed to make a record of their work for business transactions.

If the Phoenicians invented the alphabet, the Greeks added something new and important around the eighth century BC: vowels. They had a profound effect on how people viewed the world because the addition of vowels transformed writing. With vowels, the written word matched the spoken word, and its meaning, more precisely. This enhanced sense of precision helped the Greeks to better articulate rational thought and logical discourse. As a consequence, writing which had, until the eighth century BC, served mainly administrative, religious and commercial functions, became, with the use of vowels, a more useful tool and its role expanded considerably.

Around the year 1450, almost two millennia after Socrates, unusual manuscripts were impressed onto paper with the mechanical aid of the printing press—a method based on moveable type, which had appeared in the northern regions of Western Europe. This new technology was the central element in the second educational revolution: the invention of the printing press by Johann Gutenberg, the father of the modern printed book. As important as the school itself, the book opened up the world to the quick and efficient spread of knowledge and ideas. During approximately 700 years, between the fall of Rome and the twelfth century, the Church established an almost complete monopoly of book production, always in the form of manuscripts using parchment or vellum. From the end of the twelfth century, as a consequence of the social and intellectual changes and the founding of the first universities, there were transformations to the ways in which books, still using the old manuscript forms, were written, copied and distributed, were noted.

Around the fourteenth and fifteenth centuries, merchants trading with Arab countries brought in the introduction of paper, as a partial replacement for the traditional parchment or the less common vellum. This had an important effect upon book manufacture, making the production process less expensive and allowing mass volume. More than that, it was the introduction of paper into Europe that made printing possible. Initially, paper did not present the same surface qualities as parchment, but gradually won acceptance. At the end of the fourteenth century, paper was beginning to replace parchment everywhere and on entering the fifteenth century, one of the indispensable preconditions of the printed book had been realized, and paper had become a common commodity (cf., Febvre and Martin, 1958).

Since the invention and use of paper, it had become possible to manufacture large quantities of materials possessing a perfectly plain surface. It was thus an ideal medium for mass production of pictures and texts. The techniques of casting from molds and die stamping were both known from the beginning of the fifteenth century. The combination of the two techniques, by first punching out a matrix and then casting metal in it in order to obtain figures in relief, was also in use, but no one had as yet transposed this to the printing process.

Before Gutenberg, the first experiments of trying to produce a page made up of many moveable letters were unsuccessful and unable to overcome the difficulties of casting the whole page from a single mold. Gutenberg transformed the process with his invention of the press. It is still a source of great controversy as to whether Gutenberg was responsible for overcoming these technical difficulties or whether there were other

*Figure 4.2 Illustration by Gottfried-Történelmi Krónika (1908). Printing Press, Sixteenth Century in Germany.*

people involved. However, there is no doubt about his enormous importance in establishing and spreading the process around Europe at this time and he is recognized for this. For instance, in 1999, *Time* magazine named Gutenberg as the *Person of the Millennium*[1]. Anyway, fair or unfair (many people claim that a similar machine had already been invented in China one century before), for the first time in history ideas were literally put in the hands of the general public, enabling knowledge, thought and culture to spread at a rate faster than ever before (see Figure 4.2, an example of the first printing press).

## 4.3 DIGITAL TECHNOLOGIES

The third educational revolution was activated by the invention of digital technologies. The use of these new technologies allowed new forms of representation to be developed. Digital technologies are underpinned by a HyperTextual model of representation in which the introduction of new media, in particular the World Wide Web, is acting to reconfigure discursive arrangements and the place of the reader (and thus by implication the learner) within them. Conventional models of textual production and consumption have privileged the writer over the reader. The World Wide Web has created the possibility, although it is in its infancy, of a more democratic relationship to the power of textual production which works on us and not through us. Landow (1992: 70–71) coins the phrase "this HyperTextual dissolution of centrality". What he means by this is that new media allows the possibility of conversation rather than instruction, so that no one ideology or agenda dominates over another: "...the figure of the HyperText author approaches, even if it does not entirely merge with, that of the reader; the functions of reader and writer become more deeply intertwined with each other than ever before".

Landow (1992: 70) suggests that this comprises the merging of what has historically been two very different processes: "Today when we consider reading and writing, we probably think of them as serial processes or as procedures carried out intermittently by the same person: first one reads, then one writes, and then one reads some more". HyperText, which allows the possibility of having access to an almost infinite number of different texts produced by different authors, "creates an active, even intrusive reader, carries this convergence of activities one step closer to completion; but in so doing, it infringes on the power of the writer, removing some of it and granting it to the reader". This has significant implications for the development of pedagogic strategies and learning approaches.

During the twentieth century, film, radio, records, broadcast television, movies, audiotape, videotape, programmed learning machines, etc., were invented. Each time, they were proclaimed as radical educational transformations, or seen as the end of the school and the book as we know them. In reality, their impact was minimal—the dominant modes of exchange at the beginning of twenty-first century are still face-to-face discussions and paper/print resources. However, digital technologies do have the potential to affect two important elements of the teaching/learning processes: *knowledge management* and *content management*. Knowledge management is understood as the process of converting information into useful knowledge. Content management refers to the process of publishing information. Thus, high levels of knowledge and skills are required by both provider and user in a digital learning environment in order to provide efficient knowledge and content management. In this sense, digital technology competence or digital literacy are skills as necessary as writing and reading competencies used to be. Digital literacies, referring to the ability to locate, organize, understand, evaluate and analyse information using digital technologies, operate within an environment of fast developing practices, reflecting the many ways that humans interact with technologies, and in the process impacting on their innovatory capabilities.

The way knowledge is initially produced and transformed is changing rapidly, and this implies a new educational revolution in developing new teaching and learning technologies and approaches. Students who grow up in the digital age, representing the first real generation totally embedded in an environment of intelligent systems and digitized information, will learn in different ways, and will require different forms of motivation. In other words, in a digital world a key question is: "how do we motivate students to learn and teachers to teach?".

Debates concerning leaner motivation in general are complex. However, the concepts of intrinsic and extrinsic motivation that are frequently used are helpful in this context, and we draw on these key terms in the analysis which follows. *Extrinsic motivation* is governed by the goals, values and interests of others as they affect the individual learner, and participation in the activity is driven by the prospect of an external, tangible reward. Motivation, when it is externally sourced, is defined then as "engaging in an activity as a means to an end. Individuals who are extrinsically motivated work on tasks because they believe that participation will result in desirable outcomes, such as reward, teacher praise, or avoidance of punishment" (Pintrich and Schunk, 1996: 33). Note how the source of motivation here can be either negative or positive. It is, in short, where a need which is related to the learning activity, but is not fulfilled by the learning itself, is satisfied. On the other hand, *intrinsic motivation* is an engagement in an activity for its own sake. The learner is less likely to be driven by an incentive or reward other than an innate interest in the subject material itself. The consensus of the many research studies that have been conducted about motivation is that intrinsic forms of motivation are more powerful and more effective than output and external models of motivation.

Psychologists have conducted a number of experiments to determine the efficacy and effectiveness of these two forms of motivation; in other words, whether professional learners work better if motivated by tangible rewards, such as a financial bonus (i.e., external motivation) or by finding intrinsic meaning in their work (i.e., internal motivation). One pioneer of this approach was the psychologist Karl Duncker (1945) using a puzzle called *The Candle Problem*. In this experiment, the learner (or professional worker) is brought to a room where there is a table close to a wall. The learner is given some thumbtacks in a box and some matches. The challenge is to attach a candle to the wall so that the wax does not drip on to the table, without moving the table. Early attempts to solve the problem included attaching the candle to the wall by melting the wax on the side of the candle and then holding it to the wall until the wax hardened. This proved to be unsuccessful because the weight of the candle was such that the wax base quickly broke off. The solution was to see the box not only as a receptacle for the thumbtacks but also as a possible platform for the candle.

Sam Glucksberg (1962) conducted a similar experiment to show (or measure) the power of incentives, and he initially recruited people to solve the candle problem. They were divided into two groups. One group was rewarded; the other was not. The results were remarkable, with the rewarded group taking three and a half times longer to solve the problem than the non-rewarded group. This same experiment has been replicated over and over again with the same results. Daniel H. Pink (2009) has explored this and other interesting experiments to demonstrate that, while many businesses operate under the belief that the key to motivating workers is giving them tangible rewards, it seems to be an established fact that optimal performance comes when people find intrinsic meaning in their work.

This has implications for how we learn and what we learn. The introduction of digital technologies into the learning process profoundly changes it. Learners, it is suggested, are more likely to succeed if they had previously developed the skills and capacities to find answers to knowledge problems, rather than having that knowledge readily at hand. This is what we mean by digital literacy, and it empowers in three particular ways: it allows the individual to perform better in the practice; it enhances and develops the workings of the practice itself; and it enables the practice to be transformed. This also implies a new role for the teacher; that of supporting the learner or scaffolding the learning process, so that the digitally literate learner can operate independently in the practice.

In preparing students for operating in an innovatory environment, independence in thought and deed is a key element. We close this chapter by suggesting a number of key areas for investigation in this new world:

1. The process of becoming an educated person is now more complex, and thus new teaching and learning approaches and technologies have to be developed to accommodate this complexity.
2. Autonomy in learning is now central to becoming digitally literate.
3. Dispositional learning is important for the learner to cope with the new complexities in the world.
4. Models of learning in digital environments need to be underpinned by a theory of learning.
5. Any theory of learning should include a set of strategies for its effective implementation, such as in the *Assessment for Learning* schema (cf., Black *et al.*, 2003). This can be presented as five key strategies and one cohering idea. The five key strategies are: (1) engineering effective classroom discussions, questions, and learning tasks; (2) clarifying and sharing learning intentions and criteria for success; (3) providing feedback that moves learners forward (see also Hattie and Timperley, 2007 on the power of feedback); (4) activating students as the owners of their own learning; and (5) activating students as instructional resources for one another. The cohering idea is that the evidence about student learning is used to adapt instruction to better meet learning needs; in other words, that teaching is *adaptive* to the student's learning needs.
6. These five key strategies and one cohering idea need to be adapted for learning in digital environments.
7. Assessment for learning is more important than assessment of learning; indeed, the over-examined life does not necessarily lead to the educated person (Taylor, 2012).

In the next chapter we examine the relationship between education and innovation.

## NOTE

1. See Time Magazine, issue December 31, 1999, vol. 154, No. 27. Available at: http://www.time.com/time/magazine/0,9263,7601991231,00.html. Accessed August 2012.

# CHAPTER 5

# Education and Innovation

*There's a way to do it better; find it!*
(Thomas Edison, 1847–1931)[1]

In Chapter 3 we referred to the process of knowledge construction and suggested that broadly there were two forms. Gibbons *et al.* (1994) have characterized these old and new types of knowledge development as two modes: disciplinary forms of knowledge normally produced by the academy, and trans-disciplinary forms of knowledge normally produced outside it. Mode One knowledge is linear, causal, cumulative, disciplinary, reductionist and has significant status in society. Gibbons and colleagues claim that this has recently been challenged by Mode Two forms of knowledge, where technology is understood as autonomous and able to develop outside of the academy, and where it is trans-disciplinary, problem-solving, workplace-based, synoptic rather than reductionist, heterarchical and transient.

This bifurcated division has been criticized for its outmoded characterization of the academy as exclusively disciplinary, homogeneous, hierarchical, form-preserving, and its marginalization of new developments in knowledge production within universities, alongside the consolidation of older and more conventional forms. For example, Scott *et al.* (2004) identify four types of knowledge production: *disciplinarity*, *technical rationality*, *dispositionality*, and *criticality*. Disciplinarity is characterized by an indifference to the practice setting; theorizing is about the practice setting but is detached from it. Technical rationality prioritizes outsider knowledge over practice-based knowledge with the practitioner acting in a technicist manner. Dispositionality identifies certain virtues such as reflection about ends and means and even meta-reflective processes that are taught in the university and applied in the workplace. With criticality, practitioners develop the capacity to reflect critically on the discourses, and practices of the workplace of which they are members where their intention is to change them.

These forms are different manifestations of how knowledge is developed in society, and has direct implications for developing pedagogies that focus on innovatory practices, skills and dispositions. Working creatively in what has come to be known as the knowledge economy, or more accurately should be known as the knowledge sector of the economy, has meant that innovation and innovatory practices in work are a prerequisite for the success of the sector. In particular, these innovation technologies (IvTs) are now digitally mediated, using techniques such as modelling, simulating, prototyping and visualizing. Dodgson *et al.* (2005:1) identify some of the characteristics of innovation and innovatory practices: "(w)e argue that innovation may be to technology what play is to work: a possibility to break free through prescribed controlled environments and offer a temporary relaxation of rules in order to explore new alternatives". Innovation in its most basic form is the successful application of ideas; however, this is to conflate the end result with the process. We want to suggest that it is both an end result and a process, involving dispositions, values, ways of working and life orientations. (Dispositions are relatively stable habits of mind and body, sensitivities to occasion and participation repertoires, that is going on in the practice.) It is therefore not just restricted to the workplace, although it is here that it is more commonly located.

Figure 5.1 depicts Science (personified by Devotion, Labor, Truth, Research and Intuition) and Religion (personified by Purity, Faith, Hope, Reverence and Inspiration) in harmony, presided over by the central

*Figure 5.1 Stained glass window by Louis Comfort Tiffany (1890), located in Linsly-Chittenden Hall at Yale University. The centre third of "Education" window.*

personification of "Light Love Life". This suggests that creative and innovatory processes can coexist with rational processes of knowledge-development, social planning and policy formulation. Indeed, both are required in combination for constructing creative and innovatory practices.

Innovation has the following features:

- It is a deliberate, temporary relaxation of rules, norms and arrangements of resources in order to explore the possibilities of alternatives.
- It is experimental and therefore is likely to have a high rate of failure.
- It comprises the re-visualization, re-modelling, re-representation and imaginative re-formation of everyday objects and practices.
- It encourages and legitimizes exploration across epistemic, ethical, disciplinary and practice boundaries.
- It has the potential to expand understandings of the self and others, and allow self-representations of past, future and counterfactual possibilities.
- It allows the development of fictional worlds and understandings of how these might impact on life worlds and the lifecourse.
- It is a trans-disciplinary, problem-solving, heterarchical and transient knowledge-producing activity.
- It has the potential to expand understandings of the possible functions and uses of an object.
- It is the successful application of ideas.

When we imagine something, we first of all form an image or mental representation of it. However, this is different from those everyday acts of perceiving, remembering or believing, and these are different because they refer to real worlds rather than imaginary or virtual worlds. Creativity or innovation then is an imaginative act, which involves the generation of new products or ideas or the transformation of those that already exist. Chavez (2004) in relation to this, has developed an association-integration-elaboration-communication phenomenological model of creativity. The first stage of this process is associational where previously unrelated inner and outer experiences are consciously brought together to form new associations amongst sensations, thoughts, memories, ideas and emotions. This is the association-integration stage. It has been described as an incubatory process, involving a conscious and playful combining of elements (cf., Torrance and Safter, 1999).

The second stage is the elaboration stage, and this is where this playful and imaginative combining of the elements is transformed into real work and real products. In other words, the associations are made concrete. The final element is the dissemination stage where the work or product is shared, and during this process, adapted, transformed and elaborated to fit the actual conditions of the world. What is required throughout the three stages is a style of thinking that is more divergent than convergent, so that correct answers are in the first instance put to one side, as the early processes focus on the imaginative reconstruction of the possibilities relating to the self, a process or a product. In later stages of the process, the thinking becomes more convergent, as the focus is now on solutions to real-life problems. Although a pedagogical or learning element is implicit within the process, there is also a need to learn how to operate through an association-integration-elaboration-communication phenomenological model of creativity. This need is further compounded by the widespread use of digital technologies in learning environments, and thus processes of imaginative reconstruction, future problem solving, creative role playing and the elaboration of connections between ideas are mediated through systems that allow portability, flexibility, transferability, inter-changeability, enhanced student autonomy, hypertextuality, meta-cognitive awareness, and information storage and retrieval (see Chapter 6).

## 5.1 CURRICULUM MATTERS

To better understand the incorporation of new technologies in the classroom and new innovation pedagogies, at whichever sector or level of the education system, we should remember the exaggerated claims, the previously unfulfilled promises, the false expectations, and the successes and achievements of the last century's "digital technologies older cousins". These include movies, radio and television. For example, at the beginning of the 1920s, Thomas Edison predicted that the motion picture would be destined to revolutionize the educational system and that it would supplant, if not entirely replace, the use of text books. Just thirty years later, it became clear that films had not had a major impact on education, despite their huge popularity as an entertainment activity (Cuban, 1986). Radio was also heralded as *the new educational technology*, with the capacity to radically change the nature of educational institutions by transmitting to large numbers of students in the most remote areas, at negligible cost. However, a few decades later, it became obvious that the overall impact was quite modest compared with the original expectations.

These new technologies were generally well-received by teachers in classrooms, even if their impact was modest in transforming the educational environment. The reasons for the relative failure of these technologies included: the cost of equipment; the poor quality of teacher training with respect to the introduction of these new technologies; the relative incompatibility of the transmitted content with the actual school curriculum; the inappropriate quality of programming; various forms of technophobia and teachers' resistance to the in-service top-down methods of training being employed (cf., Mota, 2008, 2009b). These experiences of innovation suggest that the introduction of new technologies into complex pedagogic settings always requires systematic and institutional reforms, as well as technical ones. However, there is some evidence to suggest that the introduction of digital technologies has been more successfully achieved. The reason for this optimism is that digital technologies are more comprehensive, multi-modal, integrative and invasive than older technologies. Modern devices can cope with all the different types of media and coordinate the different functions associated with telephone, television, radio, camera, localization instruments and gaming technologies.

The school curriculum in both Brazil and England is changing over time and in response to successive waves of educational reforms in both countries. However, a feature of these reforms is a move away from a curriculum based purely on cognitive concerns, to a curriculum that hasn't abandoned such concerns—but now in addition, is more likely to focus on intrapersonal and interpersonal dispositions[2]. The cognitive domain includes three clusters of competencies: cognitive processes and strategies, knowledge and creativity. These clusters include competencies such as critical thinking, information literacy, reasoning and argumentation, and innovation (Yeager and Walton, 2011). The intrapersonal domain comprises, in turn, three clusters of competencies: intellectual openness, a work ethic and conscientiousness, and a positive core self-evaluation. These clusters include competencies such as flexibility, initiative, appreciation of diversity, and metacognition. Metacognition is associated with a sophisticated ability to reflect on one's own learning and make adjustments accordingly[3]. The interpersonal domain includes two clusters of competencies: teamwork, collaboration and leadership—which demand competencies such as communication, collaboration, responsibility—and conflict resolution[4]. These interpersonal competencies are those associated with communicating information to others, and also with interpreting others' messages and their ability to respond appropriately.

Knowledge is understood as not just information. On the contrary, information only becomes knowledge after students have interacted with that information, using it to solve problems, answer questions, or discuss interpretations. It thus becomes feasible to integrate content with method, dissolving the division between content and process. Knowledge is then connected to students' prior knowledge and schemata for making sense of the world. Interdisciplinary approaches are key to the development of these new forms of knowledge, as artificial disciplinary boundaries can restrict and reduce the capacity to operate in innovatory ways. In a world where interdisciplinarity is increasingly becoming more important, the radical separation of schools of education from schools of arts and sciences within the university, contributes to a disconnect between content and method courses.

The possibilities generated by digital technologies allow new opportunities for sharing ideas, restructuring concepts, discussing and correcting misconceptions and constructing understandings. The site can also be used to challenge student conceptions, suggesting experiments and simulations, and including provocative readings and debates. At the same time, the site, as a virtual environment, is a permanent space for discussion between students and the teacher. The material posted on the site during the interval between one classroom activity and the next represents a rich opportunity to make the classes more dynamic, allowing the teacher to correct concepts and to promote conceptual changes, advancing beyond what the student already knows. The site, under the supervision of the teacher, is the virtual collective and cooperative space where students explore problems as a small community of learners. Alongside the process of enabling students to understand and use curriculum content, the learning process itself is also a goal.

This is especially relevant because the method incorporated in the process of learning contains the main ingredients to create the stimulus for independent learning.

## 5.2 TEACHERS AS DESIGNERS

We have suggested above that innovatory and creative approaches to work and life are characterized by a number of elements: a temporary relaxation of rules; exploring the possibilities of working to alternative rules; experimenting in real-life settings; working with and not in opposition to a rational agenda; encouraging the visualization of other possibilities; applying ideas in the world; adopting trans-disciplinary, problem-solving, workplace-based, synoptic rather than reductionist, heterarchical and transient approaches to knowledge-development; and expanding the possible functionalities of objects. We have also suggested that the knowledge, skills and dispositions that are required for the development of these attributes constitute the pedagogic dimension to learning.

But first, it is incumbent on us to sketch out a theory of learning, which fits with the desire to develop creative and innovatory dispositions. Here are some suggestions: the students find out for themselves rather than being given answers to problems; the students are required to engage in a series of interrogative processes with regard to texts, people and objects in the learning environment; the students are also required to use the skills of information retrieval, information synthesis and analysis, and knowledge organization. The students may come up with inadequate, incorrect and faulty syntheses and analyses. However, this is acceptable because learning resides in the process rather than in the end-product. Learning involves the students in judging their own work against a curriculum standard and engaging in meta-processes of learning (i.e., an understanding about their own learning; the development of learning pathways; the utilization of formative assessment processes; the development of personal learning strategies; and an internalization of the curriculum). Talk (in real-life or digital formats) that is not dominated by the teacher is an essential pre-requisite of effective learning, and thus the teacher's role is to organize activities that promote talk; this involves open-ended questioning. The teacher acts as a facilitator of the process and not as the giver of information, or even as a knowledge organizer. The teacher needs to share learning intentions and success criteria with the learner; a prior articulation of a standard is an important step in effective learning. A pedagogic standard (i.e., approach, technology, series of activities) is derived from a curriculum standard. The pedagogic standard might include: task setting; negotiation with the student about appropriate ways to meet the standard; guidance about the contours of the task; and providing information to the learner on his or her performance to a standard (i.e., feedback).

A comparison between innovative pedagogic modes and traditional didactic ones can be expressed in the following way (see Table 5.1), and in relation to a set of curriculum markers which differentiate one curriculum from another: its pedagogic arrangements; the types of relations it adopts between knowledge domains; whether it is orientated towards knowledge, skill or dispositional domains; how it frames knowledge; its progression and pacing mode; the types of relations it sanctions between the teacher and his or her students; the types of relations it sanctions between learners; its spatial arrangements; its temporal arrangements; and the type of criteria it uses to evaluate whether it is successful or not.

Computer-supported innovative and transformative learning collectively offers a wide range of learning activities that could be supported through mobile digital tools and environments: exploring real physical environments linked to digital guides; investigating real physical

**Table 5.1 Comparison between Innovative and Traditional Didactic Pedagogic Modes**

|  | Traditional Approaches | Innovative Pedagogies |
|---|---|---|
| Pedagogic arrangements | Didactic | Inquiry-based |
| Relations between knowledge domains | Strong Insulation | Weak Insulation |
| Knowledge or skill/disposition orientation | Knowledge | Knowledge and Skill/Disposition |
| Knowledge frame | Strong | Weak |
| Progression and pacing | Strong | Weak |
| Relations between teacher and taught | Strongly Insulated | Weakly Insulated |
| Relations between types of learners | Strongly Insulated | Weakly Insulated |
| Spatial arrangements | Strongly Marked | Weakly Marked |
| Temporal arrangements | Strongly Marked | Weakly Marked |
| Criteria for evaluation | Explicit and Specific | Implicit and Unspecific |

environments linked to digital guides; discussing with peers, synchronously or asynchronously, audio or text; recording, capturing data related to sounds, images, videos, texts and locations; building, making and modelling, using captured data and digital tools; sharing captured data, digital products of building and modelling; testing the products built against others' products, others' comments, or real physical environments; adapting the products developed, in light of feedback; and reflecting guided by digital collaborative software, using shared products, test results, and comments (cf., Laurillard, 2002).

Laurillard's conversational framework (2002) is a dialogic teaching and learning model, which in the first instance, differentiates between what she calls the discursive level, with a focus on theories, concepts and descriptions; and an experiential level, where the focus is on practical activities, procedures and protocols. Both of these levels are interactive, but at the discursive level the interaction takes a stratified hierarchical form, where the teacher dominates in the exchange, and frames, and thus circumscribes what can be learnt and how it can be learnt. In contrast, at the experiential level, the interaction is adaptive and heterarchical. Here the student acts in the practical environment to meet a goal, and adapts and transforms his or her behaviour and understanding in the pursuit of this goal. In addition, at the experiential level the student develops theories, models and abstractions from his or her experience, and this is likely to have a beneficial effect on learning and subsequent behaviour. In a similar fashion, at the discursive level, the student benefits from reflecting on his or her experiences. For the teacher, there is a similar process. The teacher constructs a suitable learning environment and in the process is engaged in a learning activity, and at the discursive level, his or her deliberations are enhanced by reflecting on the students' performance at the experiential level. Further to this, at the experiential level, feedback between peers influences their output from actions on the environment.

Laurillard's Conversational Framework is designed to act as a framework for supporting the learning process. For example, it claims that: "learners may be motivated to think about the theory if they have to use it in order to act in the environment to achieve the task goal; their motivation to practise repeated actions will be higher if the feedback on their action is intrinsic (i.e., showing the result of their action in such a way that it is clear how to improve it); and they will be motivated more to reflect on that experience if they are required to produce some version of their own idea to the teacher at the discursive level—this would traditionally be an essay, or a report, or a model, depending on the discipline" (Laurillard, 2002: 34). Similarly, in relation to peer collaboration, she claims that: "learners will be motivated to improve their practice if they can share their outputs with peers; and will be motivated to improve their practice and augment their conceptual understanding if they can reflect on their experience by discussing their outputs with peers" (Laurillard, 2002: 35).

In a later work, Laurillard (2012) argues that teachers should be seen as design scientists and this requires the development of a knowledge field appropriate to representing, testing and sharing educational designs. Further to this, Laurillard argues that the appropriate use of digital technologies should allow teachers to go beyond them, rather than just sharing teaching approaches and designs developed through open educational resources (Santos, 2011) or traditional journals, reviews and conference proceedings. Laurillard and McAndrew (2009) also use the concept of a pedagogical pattern, which is "to develop a way to articulate, test and to share the principles and practice of teaching that builds our knowledge of how to use digital technologies". In this sense, by attaching that format to pedagogy as a means to facilitate formal learning, it makes pedagogical patterns different from generic design patterns, from technical learning designs, and also from less structured learning patterns (McAndrew et al., 2006).

Following Laurillard's ideas (2008, 2012), pedagogical patterns go beyond and are more than a sequence of teaching-learning activities. They are able to link to learning principles by articulating the practice of teaching and capturing the pedagogy that a teacher has found to be most effective. A detailed discussion is available in Laurillard (2012), about how to capture and represent a teacher's effective pedagogical ideas in the form of pedagogical patterns. A teaching method template describes a teaching design in terms of: "general categories, such as summary, rationale, learning outcomes, duration, group size, learner characteristics, and setting; detailed teaching information, such as sequence of activities, roles, assessment method, resources, references; and comment sections, such as teacher reflection, student feedback, and peer review". The pedagogical patterns, resulting from this approach of teaching as a design science, allow the teacher to share his or her pedagogic ideas in such a way that other colleagues who might consider adopting a new pattern would know its origin, and should be able to track the way it was developed. In addition, as long as users are stimulated to contribute, they can have their contributions acknowledged, preserving their intellectual property rights in a similar way to citations in traditional research.

## 5.3 MASSIVE OPEN ONLINE COURSES

Massive Open Online Course (MOOC) is a recent phenomenon in the area of distance education and very closely associated with independent learning ideals. Ken[5] has suggested that it is one of the most important experiments in higher education teaching and learning, and may qualify as an inflection point for online teaching and learning approaches. MOOCs are relatively new and at a developmental stage; new forms are emerging and new types are being used. The two principal features of MOOCs are *open access* and *scalability*. Participants, indeed active learners, do not have to be registered on a permanent basis and they are not required to pay the normal fee. In addition, MOOCs are designed to support a large number of enrolments.

Ivan Illich was an enthusiastic pioneer. Almost half a century ago, he was arguing for openness in education and the use of computers in the learning process as a way to contribute to reforming education systems, which, at the beginning of the 1970s, he referred to as "broken" (Illich, 1973). He died in 2002, before the development of the first MOOCs. Although online courses in higher education have been offered since the mid-1990s, it is generally accepted that the first MOOC, or proto-MOOC, was taught by David Wiley at Utah State University in August 2007. The term "MOOC" was coined 1 year later by Dave Cormier at the University of Prince Edward Island and George Siemens at University of Manitoba in Canada[6].

Even though it was competing with many other similar initiatives at the end of the last decade, MOOCs only gained significant public attention when Stanford University's artificial intelligent course in the autumn 2011 semester attracted nearly 160,000 students. More recently, two Stanford professors created a for-profits company (although currently not generating revenue) named Coursera[7]. Coursera consists of a platform of elite international universities, including, among others, Princeton, École Polytechnique Fédérale de Lausanne, the Universities of Toronto, Columbia, Brown, Melbourne, the Hebrew University of Jerusalem and the Hong Kong University of Science and Technology. Coursera offers more than one hundred MOOCs across dozens of categories ranging from engineering to sociology, and this initiative is committed to making the best education in the world freely available to any person who seeks it. The more than 1 million enrolments come from 196 countries, with a concentration of almost 40% from the United States but with significant contributions (around 5% each) from other countries like Brazil, India, China and Canada.

Other important initiatives are flourishing; for instance, the Massachusetts Institute of Technology (MIT) started a free class project, MITx2[8] in December 2011. At the beginning of 2012, a Stanford professor who also helped teach the artificial intelligence class founded Udacity3[9], a company offering free courses in partnership with colleges. In May 2012, Harvard University together with MIT and the University of Berkeley created a similar venture, edX4[10]. The pedagogy behind a MOOC is based on connectivism, which is a theory of learning for the digital age that is usually understood as contrasting with traditional behaviourist, cognitivist, and constructivist approaches (Kop, 2011). Connectivism is more than just self-directed learning, as connectivism is more than students learning at their own pace and interest. Connectivism is understood as learning in complex environments, based on networks, which are shaped, influenced, and directed by the many ways we are connected to others, relying on social, technological and informational nodes to direct the educational activities.

MOOCs also encourage a form of independent learning, with the following features: learning and knowledge-development are contested activities; learning is a process of connecting specialized nodes or information sources; learning may reside in non-human appliances; learning is prospective so that it is more important to realize that there is more knowledge than is currently codified; nurturing and maintaining connections are needed to facilitate continuous learning; and the ability to make connections between fields, ideas and concepts is a core skill. The associated basic procedures that characterize MOOCs include: *aggregation* where, in opposition to traditional courses with their static content and *a priori* definition, new content is permanently placed on the accessible web page, based on interactivity between teachers and students; *remixing* so that the materials specifically designed for the course are integrated with any other appropriate available materials; *customization* where the resulting material is continuously redesigned in a customized form, that can then be properly utilized for each participant to achieve his or her targets; and *sharing* where the redesigned material can be shared with other participants.

According to Phil Hill[11], the most important barriers that MOOCs must overcome to build a sustainable model are: developing revenue models to make the concept self-sustaining; delivering valuable signifiers of completion such as credentials, badges or acceptance into accredited programmes; low course completion rates, as most MOOCs today have less than 10% of registered students actually completing the course; and authenticating students in a manner to satisfy an accreditation institution or hiring company that is known to the student. Nevertheless, the benefits for the learner by adopting MOOCs as a source for knowledge are significant, and explain, at least partially, their recent success:

- MOOCs are open, even for those not attached to the specific institution promoting the course and, in general, free for all.
- Their flexibility of use allows participants to operate independently of space and time.
- There is no formal curriculum, and thus students are not constrained by the demands of following a programme of learning.
- They allow a greater degree of sharing ideas and additional material with participants than is available on traditional courses.
- The equipment required to access the material and internet connectivity is becoming increasingly available.
- There are many opportunities for links to previous contents, depending on the specific student level or interest.
- There is a wide variety of assignments to choose from, allowing student customization in accordance with the student profile or the particular demand.
- They are relatively low cost for teachers, and can be developed collaboratively.
- MOCCs can be developed for work-based purposes, allowing employees to attend even during the hours of work.

- They take account of the way our lives are increasingly becoming ones of digital immersion.
- They allow networking between and by teachers.

There are at least two current types of MOOCs in the market. According to George Siemens[12], the two principal branches are the cMOOCs (CCK-style MOOCs), and the xMOOCs, like Coursera and EDx. The first model presents the content as a starting point and learners are expected interactively to create content. This is treated as an open educational resource, content is distributed, often blog-based and in other learner-created forums and spaces, and there is a radically different relationship between teachers and learners. The second model is more traditional, in that the MOOC is understood as a structured course where learners are expected to master what they are taught, with content provision, a centralized discussion forum support, and traditional relationships between teachers and learners. At the moment, MOOCs are still in a developmental stage. The MOOCs have not offered traditional credits, just a "statement of accomplishment" and, sometimes, a grade. However, the University of Washington[13] is now preparing to offer credit for its next Coursera MOOC, and students will probably have to pay a fee for the extra assignments, instructors etc. Almost certainly, MOOCs will take on different pedagogic forms and be received differently by students. For many, the marginalization of curriculum concerns, and their lack of a strong epistemological base, means that they are treated with some scepticism by the educational community.

## 5.4 TEACHING FOR INNOVATION

Teachers are becoming designers, courses are becoming MOOCs, times are changing fast and the industrial revolution is long gone, as well as the standard of teaching following a set routine or previously defined format. Teachers increasingly have to prepare students for a world that is unknown, and for jobs that probably do not exist. This requires an appropriate pedagogy and a clear understanding about the role the new digital technologies can play in the educational process.

One of the most interesting examples of these new technologies is the electronic book, digital book or simply e-book[14]. The e-book is an electronic version of a printed book, published in digital form, consisting of text, images, audio, etc., and produced and used on computers, portable devices, some handsets or other digital devices. It usually comes with tools that can make reading easier compared to a normal book. The e-book is a relatively new phenomenon, but its influence continues to grow within the literary world (Gardiner and Musto, 2010). What makes the e-book so attractive is the real possibility for the book to become adaptive and dynamic. It means that teachers can provide alternative versions in text or as graphic, video or audio elements, and it can be customized for each particular situation. Hypertextual processes are provided and easily utilized. It is designed in a way that its visualization, downloading and usage become handier and cheaper than a printed book. The students will be able to co-read, sharing the text with others, including the tutor, reading the same material, and able to discuss its content.

Manuals and technical documents were the earliest e-books and written for specific groups with a limited interest. More recently, e-book subjects and formats have increased in popularity and availability. New models and technology continue to be developed, but nowadays there are, at least, three main e-reader technologies that currently dominate the market: Amazon's *Kindle*, Sony's *PRS-500* and *Cybook Gen3* (*Bookeen*). Additionally, in January 2010, Apple launched the *iPad*, on which e-books can also be read[14]. One important reference for the e-book was the Gutenberg Project[15] launched by Michael S. Hart in 1971, designed to *encourage the creation and distribution of eBooks*. Project Gutenberg is actually a public library full of digital books. It houses a collection of thousands of books, including a great number of the classics. At the same time, the operators of the Xerox Sigma V mainframe had given Michael S. Hart an operator's account with US$100 million of computer time in it at the Materials Research Lab at the University of Illinois. Nevertheless, only twenty years later, the first enterprise, the *Book Stacks Unlimited*, began selling new books online. In 1993, the first software to read digital books was developed—*Digital Book v.1*. In 1995, Amazon started to sell books online. The first ISBN issued on an e-book and marketing was on e-books on CDs in 1998.

The main reason why higher education students are adopting e-books is the benefits associated with the convenience, availability and portability of course texts and supplementary materials. However, there are surveys[14] suggesting that students are demanding a new generation of e-books that should overcome some of the existing limitations (web pages to open simultaneously, to take notes directly and book marking, to study in the group by sharing information, etc.) and technical problems. The most recent dynamic books[16] allow a group of students to read, annotate and compare texts, sharing the experience up to the point that it is possible to comment online on what is being created by colleagues. Additionally, they are less expensive than traditionally printed textbooks and immediately available for access. Consequently, new forms of teaching and learning based on dynamic e-books are possible through shared and collaborative pedagogies. Functions built into the devices (like camera, video, voice recorder, GPS locator, timer, etc.) allow experiments to be conducted directly with data storage and the use of graphs and tables in many different areas (Fomel and Claerbout, 2009). From the point of view of instructors, dynamic books have the possibility of customizing existing textbooks, combining up-to-date material with material which is specifically designed to meet students' needs. It allows some measure of control over course content, including adding, deleting and rearranging chapters and sections from a variety of textbooks. These can be done in such a way that the new contributions can be highlighted, avoiding confusion between the original version and what has been added to it.

In this chapter we have suggested that innovatory and creative approaches to work and life are characterized by a number of elements: a temporary relaxation of rules; exploring the possibility of working to alternative rules; experimenting in real-life settings; working with and not in opposition to a rational agenda; encouraging the visualization of other possibilities; applying ideas in the world; adopting trans-disciplinary, problem-solving, workplace-based, synoptic rather than reductionist, heterarchical and transient approaches to knowledge-development; and expanding the possible functionalities of objects. We have also suggested that the knowledge, skills and dispositions that are required for the development of these attributes constitute the pedagogic dimension to learning. We have begun the process of working out what these might be; indeed, we have begun the process of developing a theory of e-learning, and in the next chapter we take this process one stage further.

## NOTES

1. As seen at http://www.duxinaroe.com/1/post/2012/08/theres-a-way-to-do-it-better-find-it-thomas-edison.html. Accessed October 2012.

2. National Research Council. (2011). *Assessing 21st century skills: Summary of a workshop.* Koenig, Rapporteur. Committee on the Assessment of 21st Century Skills. Board on Testing and Assessment, Division of Behavioral and Social Sciences and Education. Washington, D.C.: National Academies Press. Available at: http://www.nap.edu/catalog.php?record_id = 13215. Accessed August 2012.

3. Hoyle, R.H. and Davisson, E.K. *Assessment of self-regulation and related constructs: Prospects and challenges,* paper prepared for the NRC Workshop on Assessment of 21st Century Skills, 2011. Available at: http://www.nap.edu/openbook.php?record_id = 13215&page = 63. Accessed August 2012.

4. Salas, E., Bedwell, W.L., and Fiore, S.M. *Developing the 21st century (and beyond) workforce: A review of interpersonal skills and measurements strategies,* paper prepared for the NRC Workshop on Assessing 21st Century Skills, 2011. Available at: http://www.nap.edu/openbook.php?record_id = 13398&page = R1. Accessed August 2012.

5. Ken, M. "A brief guide to understand MOOCs". *The Internet Journal of Medical Education,* 1 (2011). As seen at: http://archive.ispub.com/journal/the-internet-journal-of-medical-education/volume-1-number-2/a-brief-guide-to-understanding-moocs.html#sthash.I3grDBts.dpbs. Accessed January 2013.

6. Available at: http://www.youtube.com/watch?v = -a2cEzsMEMY. Accessed October 2012.

7. Available at: http://www.crunchbase.com/company/coursera. Accessed October 2021

8. Available at: http://ocw.mit.edu/index.htm. Accessed October 2012.

9. Available at: http://www.udacity.com. Accessed October 2012.

10. Available at: https://www.edx.org. Accessed October 2012.

11. Available at: http://mfeldstein.com/four-barriers-that-moocs-must-overcome-to-become-sustainable-model/. Accessed October 2012.

12. Available at: http://www.slideshare.net/gsiemens/designing-and-running-a-mooc. Accessed October 2012.

13. As seen at: http://www.whitehouse.gov/issues/education/k-12/educate-innovate/. Accessed October 2012.

14. Sharples, M., McAndrew, P., Weller, M. *et al.* Open University, Innovation Report 1. Innovation Pedagogy 2012. Available at: http://www.open.ac.uk/blogs/innovating/. Accessed October 2012.

15. Available at: http://www.gutenberg.org/. Accessed October 2012.

16. Available at: http://www.dynamicbooks.com. Accessed October 2012.

# CHAPTER 6

# Independent Learning: A Strategy for Innovation

*Thinking is like loving or dying. Each of us must do it for ourselves.*
(Josiah Royce, 1855–1916)[1]

In this chapter we develop a digital theory of learning. Traditionally, seven principal pedagogical approaches have been identified, although they flex and overlap with each other. The first of these is *dogmatic instruction*, and this has its origins in religious communities. Here learning comes from contemplation of a set of divinely inspired maxims about how one should live and the nature of truth. Some secular ideologies, such as Marxism–Leninism, have come to be used in the same way, so that the learning approach is based on a determination of the true and unequivocal meaning of a sacred text or set of images.

The second pedagogic mode points to a different form of expertise. Here, the authority for a set of precepts about how one should conduct oneself privately and publically comes from membership of an expert body, such as a profession, guild or speciality. This is a form of *expert credentialism*, and the teaching tool generally adopted is learning through case studies or simulations of appropriate actions in the world. The third style or pedagogic approach is what is known as *individual self-discovery*, where the learner seeks to pursue a path towards some form of ultimate satisfaction or completeness. Ron Barnett captures the process that this implies in the following way: "The *pedagogical challenge* [emphasis in the original] lies in the student's will being so formed that she wills herself to go forward into those spaces which may challenge her being itself" (Barnett, 2007: 155). Such a pursuit comprises a variety of learning modes, but is in essence experiential and its focus is on contemplation of the self.

The fourth mode of pedagogy is the *Socratic method*, which we referred to in Chapter 3. Here, a learner develops an argument about his or her fundamental beliefs in how the world works and how he or she should behave in this world. This is challenged by a mentor or teacher, who acts as a disputant. It is a form of enquiry and debate in which the learner and mentor argue from different positions by challenging the foundations of each other's argument. It is a negative method of hypothesis elimination, as better theories are developed by identifying and then discarding those which are shown to be inadequate, illogical or contradictory.

The fifth pedagogical mode is what has been called *service learning*, where the learner temporarily immerses him or herself in the work or works of the community, and in particular, in solving problems and providing solutions to social ills or difficulties. Learning becomes synonymous with living, albeit that these learning environments are carefully chosen to represent heightened or exaggerated social situations. Service learning can, however, be less structured than another long-standing approach, the sixth pedagogical mode: *learning by doing*. Practicum learning has a long and honourable tradition in professional higher education in particular, often involving supervised but live practice, and sometimes overlapping with periods of probationary service after graduation, but before full qualification.

Finally, for many, especially in the modern world, graduation may not be the sole target, or even the final outcome. Learning is understood as lifelong and of long duration. Post-compulsory education and training has become a much more flexible and ill-defined affair, achieving its goals for many through complex patterns of the seventh pedagogical mode: *life-long learning*. Here, qualifications and part-qualifications need not be sequential or connected, in subject or level. They can be chosen, or prescribed for tactical, strategic or other reasons (Schuller and Watson, 2009).

These pedagogical interventions (dogmatic instruction, expert credentialism, self-discovery, service learning, the Socratic method, learning by doing, and life-long learning), as well as their curricular content, do not map directly onto the current array of instructional environments and teaching techniques. This is particularly true for teaching and learning approaches that are mediated through new digital technologies. We have already noted that the learning episode can just as easily take place down a line and asynchronously as face-to-face. New technologies such as correspondence and broadcast were designed and utilized to attract new types of students, and these rapidly became mainstream modes of delivery in the university sector. For example, the Massachusetts Institute of Technology (MIT) has moved from simply publishing programme and course material on-line to the development of a sophisticated programme of custom-designed and interactive materials[2]; and a range of institutions have joined the Coursera Network. The latter now has over 1 million registrations (although many of them can be described as browsers), followed by its rival Udacity (home of Massive Open Online Courses, or MOOCs) with nearly three-quarters of a million[3].

In response then to these new technologies, there is an implicit demand for new teaching and learning approaches, which we might like to call independent and transformative learning pedagogies. However, we need in the first instance to understand what learning is and to develop a theory of learning. Each and every learning episode has a series of elements: a determination of the circumstances in which learning can take place in the specific environment; a set of resources and technologies to allow that learning to take place; a particular type of relationship between teacher and learner to effect that learning; a theory of learning, that is, an account of how the learning (expressed as a knowledge set, skill or disposition/inclination) can be assimilated; and a further account of how the learning which has taken place in a particular set of circumstances (for example, in an institution of higher education with a set of learners), in a particular way, with a particular theory of learning underpinning it, and so forth, can transfer to environments in other places and times (cf., Scott *et al.*, 2013).

Learning can be theorized as a process, with a range of characteristics. It has a set of pedagogic relations; that is, it incorporates a relationship between a learner and a catalyst, which could be a person, an object in nature, an artefact, a particular array of resources, an allocation of a role or function to a person, a text, or a sensory object. A change process is required, either internal to the learner or external to the community of which this learner is a member. Each learning episode has socio-historical roots. What is learnt in the first place is formed in society and outside the individual. It is shaped by the life that the person is leading. It is thus both externally and internally mediated, and the form taken is determined by whether the process is cognitive, affective, meta-cognitive, conative or expressive. Finally, learning has an internalization element, where what is formally external to the learner is interiorized by the learner, and a performative element, where what is formally internal to the learner is exteriorized by the learner in the world (*ibid.*).

## 6.1 LEARNING THEORIES

Jerome Bruner (1996) distinguishes between symbol-processing and socio-cultural views of learning. The first of these theories is the computational or symbol-processing view, where learning is understood as the sorting, storing and retrieving of coded information, and it works as a computer does. The mind is a blank screen. Information is received by the mind, and this consists of already digested facts about the world, which represent how the world works. The mind, in the act of learning, receives that information, incorporates it into its already held store of facts and theories, and then adjusts its schema or world-view in the light of this new information. This is mechanistic, algorithmic and deterministic, and although interpretation is built into the process, it is severely restricted and reductionist. Learning becomes a passive process, and if a judgement is made about these learning processes, then it is made in terms of efficiency and efficacy rather than merit.

These symbol processing approaches have their origins in the philosophical theory of empiricism, which understands the world as given and then received by individual minds. It separates out language from reality, mind from body and the individual from society (Bredo, 1999). A philosophical theory of empiricism, or its sociological manifestation, positivism, suggests that facts can be collected about the world, free of the value assumptions and belief systems of the collector. These so-called facts constitute unequivocal and true statements about the world. Furthermore, learning is conceptualized as discovering what they are and developing adequate explanations of them. However, this implies that the world is constituted by language and that participating in these language practices allows one to represent reality in a coherent way. What this also implies is that the source of understanding, learning, and indeed being, is in society and, in particular, in communities of learners located in time and place. This challenges realist assumptions that there is a world or reality out there which is separate from our knowledge of it, and that human beings have invented symbolic systems such as language and mathematical notation that mirror that reality. In contrast, there is a more radical and fundamentally different solution to the problem of the relationship between mind and reality.

These representations of reality are not given in a prior sense because of the nature of reality (i.e., metaphysical and therefore transcendental and ontological essentialisms), or because the mind is constructed in a certain way (i.e., cognitive-universalist essentialisms), but as a result of individual human beings actively constructing and reconstructing that reality in conjunction with other human beings, some contemporary, some long since dead.

These symbol-processing approaches to cognition and learning also suggest a further dualism between mind and body. This separation of mind and body, indeed, the subsequent dualism which is created, locates learning and cognition in the mind, as it passively receives information from the bodily senses, which it then processes. The mind is thought of as being separate from the material body and from the environment in which the body is located. Learning is conceptualized as a passive process of receiving information from the environment. In contrast to this, situated-cognitionists argue that learning involves interactive contact with the environment. This contributes to a further understanding for the individual, and indeed has a further effect, which is to change or transform the environment itself. In other words, knowledge is not understood as a passive body of knowledge, skills and dispositions to be acquired from the environment, but as an interactive process of construction and re-contextualization.

There is a third dualism which we need to consider: the separation of the individual from society. If a learner is given a task to complete, he or she has to figure out what the problem is and how it can be solved. The task moreover, is framed by a set of social assumptions made by the teacher. The problem with the symbol-processing view is that an assumption is made that the task, and the way it can be solved, are understood in the same way by both learner and teacher. However, this assumption should not be made, and one of the consequences of making it is that the learner who then fails to solve the problem is considered to be inadequate in some specified way, rather than someone who has reconfigured or interpreted the problem in a way which is incongruent with that of the teacher or observer. The individual/societal distinction which is central to a symbol-processing view of cognition separates out individual mental operations from the construction of knowledge by communities of people, and this leaves it incomplete as a theory of learning.

This symbol-processing or computational view of learning can be compared with learning theories that emphasize cultural aspects which are situated or embedded in society. Situated-cognition or sociocultural theories of learning view the person and the environment as mutually constructed and mutually constructing. As a result, they stress active, transformative and relational dimensions to learning; indeed, they understand learning as contextualized. This employs a Vygotskian framework and focuses on the notion of scaffolding (Vygotsky, 1978). Scaffolding in teaching essentially means an aid which is offered to the learner by a more experienced person (i.e., a teacher, mentor or pedagogic expert) in support of the learning process. Van de Pol *et al.* (2010) suggest that this difficult and contested concept has a number of characteristics: it is a temporary support; it is offered to the learner in relation to specific tasks that he or she is asked to perform; and the learner is unlikely to complete the task without it. In addition, the scaffold is provided to the learner by the teacher in his or her capacity as "expert in relation to the satisfactory completion of the task" (Sharma and Hannafin, 2007).

Wood and Wood (1996a,b) suggest that scaffolding can help to overcome task uncertainty and contingency. If the learner is unsure what a task entails, and therefore what a proper solution to the task might be, it is likely that he or she will be unable to complete it without assistance. The expert has the role of defining the features of the task for the learner, and this might include examples of how similar tasks have been completed. This allows a bridge to be built between novice and teacher. This therefore has the effect of reducing uncertainty. However, this process is not about giving an answer or a solution to the learner, which can then be reflected upon. What is internalized is a way of solving such tasks that can then be transferred to the solving of similar tasks. The second principle, contingency, provides support for the learner which is then progressively reduced until he or she is able to perform the task independently. The expert thus intervenes in the learning process in relation to the learner's needs, moving from a more structured to a less structured approach, until the learner can perform the action independently.

Despite its apparent simplicity, the broader notion of scaffolding in teaching is rather complex and its use in everyday teaching situations come with a number of qualifications. First, there is no real agreement on the definition of scaffolding and on closely related mechanisms such as "contingency", "fading", and "transfer of responsibility" (van de Pol *et al.*, 2010). Second, scaffolding is understood as a dynamic intervention which is then adjusted (for better functioning) to accommodate the learner's on-going progress. For these reasons, the amount and type of support given by the teacher depends on both the learning setting and how the student responds to the task. So, scaffolding operates differently in different situations and is not a one-size-fits-all technique. As a result, learning theorists are beginning to draw a distinction between the scaffold's means and its intentions.

The Assessment for Learning movement (Black *et al.*, 2003) has captured some of these concerns, although three criticisms can be made: (i) the focus on formative assessment has inevitably marginalized processes of learning; (ii) as a result, some of their strategies are both misapplied and misunderstood (for example, peer learning does not amount to asking students to make quantitative judgements about their colleague's work in relation to a set of criteria); and (iii) the reductive process for the purposes of quantifying and comparing results may have led to a distortion of the process of learning. Assessment for learning can be presented, as five key strategies and one cohering idea. The five key strategies are: (i) engineering effective classroom discussions, questions, and learning tasks; (ii) clarifying and sharing learning intentions and criteria for success; (iii) providing feedback that moves learners forward (Hattie and Timperley, 2007); (iv) activating students as the owners of their own learning; and (v) activating students as instructional resources for one another. The cohering idea is that evidence about student learning is used to adapt instruction to better meet learning needs; in other words, that teaching is adaptive to the student's learning needs (cf., Black *et al.*, 2003)

The key then is the relationship between the formative and developmental processes of assessment *and* learning. Torrance and Pryor (1998) have identified a range of assessment approaches with *convergent assessment* at one end of a spectrum to *divergent assessment* at the other. Convergent assessment processes require correct answers from students; whereas divergent assessment processes are more concerned to explore what students can and cannot do, and how they make connections between ideas. They suggest that divergent assessment leads to students choosing to engage with subject knowledge to a greater extent and to make new connections between ideas, while convergent assessment tends to be an end in itself. Feedback within a convergent framework focuses on the elicitation of correct answers and identifies errors in a student's performance (Black and William, 1998), while within a divergent framework, feedback is "exploratory, provisional or provocative" (Torrance and Pryor, 1998), often encouraging students to reconstruct their thinking about the subject domain or learning process.

Butler and Winne (1995) in turn, suggest that feedback is most useful when it feeds directly into a student's own monitoring system, to allow him or her to assess his or her own progress and work out what should be done next. They point to the complex and individualized nature of this important form of knowledge construction, and suggest that when students seek out or receive external feedback, this may "*confirm, add to,* or *conflict with* the learner's interpretations of the task and the path of learning" (p. 248; *our emphases*). Thus, any feedback messages given by a teacher or expert may be understood and used differently by each individual learner, and thus have a different effect on the learning process. As Hattie and Timperley (2007) suggest, if the purpose of feedback is to provoke thought about appropriate learning strategies rather than about task completion, then it can also be associated with students feeding back to themselves more effectively, and this allows them a greater measure of independence from the teacher, especially in relation to their own learning strategies. Such learners are likely to be competent in: setting or adjusting their own goals for upgrading knowledge; deliberating about strategies to select effective ones; self-monitoring the accumulating effects of engagement; managing their motivation; and adapting or inventing their own tactics for making progress (Butler and Winne, 1995). This process of auto-feedback is associated with complex learning outcomes, such as greater domain understanding and more sophisticated strategy processing (Black and William, 1998).

Learning environments are constructed in particular ways, with choices made at institutional and classroom levels about pedagogic arrangements, relations between knowledge domains, knowledge or skill orientations, the knowledge frame, progression and pacing, relations between teacher and learner, relations between types of learners, spatial arrangements, temporal arrangements, and the criteria and means of evaluation. Above all else the learning environment can be characterized by the type of learning that underpins the educational programme. In addition to our two general theories of learning, symbol processing and socio-constructivism, there are a number of specific educational theories or ideologies, such as behaviourism, cognitivism and constructivism. These directly underpin to a greater or lesser degree the construction of learning sets or sequences.

## 6.2 LEARNING FRAMEWORKS

Behaviourism is a theory of stimulus and response. The emphasis here is on modifying behaviours; and internal mental states or states of consciousness are considered to be of little importance. They are not considered relevant to the idea or practice of learning. The learner is passive, and behaviours are understood as being caused by external stimuli as operant conditions. B.F. Skinner, a leading proponent, argued the following. Pleasant experiences are positive reinforcers. If experienced by a learner, they establish connections between stimuli and response. On the other hand, unpleasant experiences are negative reinforcers. They have the effect of causing learners to avoid undesirable responses to stimuli. If learning is continuously reinforced, this increases the rate and depth of that learning. Both positive and negative reinforcement can shape behaviours immediately and in the long-term. If the learner does not receive any reinforcement, then this can also shape behaviour. If learners do not receive any response to their behaviour, they may change their behaviour to induce or encourage some kind of external reinforcement.

An example of a programme of learning underpinned by a behaviourist meta-theory is the Keller method. This method, or, more accurately, teaching and learning approach, has been influential, if not decisively successful, in the education of the professions in Brazil (Mota, 2013). The Keller Plan (Keller, 1968) was launched in the early 1960s and it is an early attempt to use new technologies in teaching and learning environments. The Plan, also called the Personalized System of Instruction (PSI), was developed by Fred S. Keller with J. Gilmour Sherman, Carolina Bori and Rodolpho Azzi, among others, in the middle 1960s as an innovative method of instruction for the then new University of Brasilia. When the Keller Plan was launched, the new digital technologies were in their infancy and this meant that content delivery, the development of learning environments, and their capacity to deliver a deep learning experience, was limited. In addition, its reliance on a behaviourist approach meant that it was operating with a severely restricted pedagogy, and consequently its impact on learning was less than originally hoped for. However, it is worth examining because it constituted an early attempt to use the new technologies to create productive learning environments.

The Keller Plan is a type of personalized instruction in which learning materials are presented in small units. When a student feels ready, they take a test prior to completing the unit and, if they pass at an appropriate level, are allowed to continue on the unit. This test is also diagnostic in that it provides a description of the capabilities of the student, which allows the subsequent programme to be adjusted to the needs of the student. It is in this sense that the programme can be described as personalized. The student completes each of the subsequent units at his or her own pace. This indicates one of the benefits of this form of learning: the capacity of the system to accommodate students who wish to progress through the programme rapidly, as well as those who wish to take their time. This is one element of the inherent flexibility in these types of teaching and learning approaches. Under the Keller Plan, instructors (or teachers as we would know them) serve only as facilitators, administer no punishment at any stage of the learning, and award only pass or fail grades.

The Keller Plan is underpinned by a behaviourist philosophy (Zimmerman, 2002). The primary presentation of new content was through written texts. Given the forms of media available at the time when the Keller Plan was developed (e.g., lectures, movies, audio records, television, radio, paper-based text, etc.), paper-based texts gave students the greatest freedom; books and texts are portable, can be read at one's own pace, can be started and stopped at any time, can be easily reviewed, and can be written upon by the reader. As an application of behaviourism, the Keller Plan was designed to maximize the number of operant behaviours that could be reinforced; this could best be done with written materials rather than learners being passive observers of other media.

Subject matter material was broken down into separable, meaningful units. These units could have various kinds of relationships; for example, one unit could provide learning which forms a prerequisite for understanding another, or a later unit could be an elaboration of an earlier one. Indeed, these forms of learning, because they allow flexibility, are able to accommodate different progression modes. A number of these progression modes have been identified. The first is prior condition. In the acquisition of particular knowledge, skill and dispositional elements, there are pre-requisites in the learning process. An example might be mathematical where knowledge of addition is a pre-requisite of multiplication. A second form is maturational. A maturational form of progression refers to the development of the mind of the learner. There are some mental operations that cannot be performed by the learner because the brain is too immature to process them. A third form is extensional. An extensional form of progression is understood as an increase in the amount, or range, of an operation. Greater coverage of the material is a form of progression, so a learner now understands more examples of the construct, or more applications of the construct, and can operate with a greater range of ideas.

A fourth form is intensification. Related to the idea of extension is a deepening or intensifying of the construct or skill. Whereas extension refers to the amount or range of progression, intensification refers to the extent to which a sophisticated understanding has replaced a superficial understanding of the concept. Then there is a notion of complexity. In relation to the knowledge constructs, skills and dispositions implicit within a learning environment, there are four forms of complexity that allow differentiation between units. These are: behavioural complexity, symbolic complexity, affective complexity and perceptual complexity. There is also a type of progression, abstracting, which involves moving from the concrete understanding of a concept to a more abstract version. A further measure of progression is an increased capacity to articulate, explain or amplify an idea or construct (i.e., learners retain the ability to deploy the skill and in addition, they can now articulate, explain or amplify what they are able to do and what they have done). A final form of progression is pedagogical, and this refers to the way that learning is also influenced by its means of delivery. An example could be moving from an assisted performance to an independent one. Students are allowed to advance through the course material at their own pace and in an order which suits the type of progression that is most appropriate for them. Learners then move through a programme as quickly or slowly as they choose, as long as they finish the whole programme within a determined period of time.

Students are required to satisfy a mastery requirement in one unit before proceeding to the next. Typically, a unit in the programme would have more than one equivalent form of assessment; for example, three quizzes of equal difficulty or three primary sources or data sets to be analysed. Students are required to demonstrate mastery of a unit's objectives at a certain level. If the student does not reach the threshold, he or she is redirected to unit materials (or supplements if provided) and can then take an equivalent form of the unit assessment. From a behaviourist perspective, demonstrating mastery, and being allowed to continue to a subsequent unit, was presumed to be reinforcing.

Teaching assistants or proctors were an important element of the Keller Plan. They could have been external to the programme (adults or peers recruited from external sources) or internal (advanced students on the programme who were doing well, had completed all the units to date, and had good interpersonal skills). They acted as the arbiters of unit mastery; they certified mastery, identified areas of weakness, and directed students to the next units. The Keller Plan was used extensively in the Brazilian higher education system, particularly as a more personalized form of instruction, but there is nothing inherent in the Keller formulation to restrict its application to particular grade levels, contents or types of programmes. There has been some research on the effectiveness of the Keller method which suggests that it has had robust, significantly positive effects on learning when compared to more traditional lecture-based formats (Pear and Crone-Todd, 1999).

The Keller Plan, as we have suggested, is underpinned by a behaviourist meta-theory and this may have contributed to its relative lack of success. Behaviourism can be contrasted with the two alternative meta-theories that we have already made reference to: *cognitivism or symbol-processing* and *constructivism*. The main focus of cognitivism is the role played by inner mental activities. The learner is viewed as an information processor, passively receiving information from an external source. Cognitivist perspectives on learning are a paradigm example of a symbol-processing learning philosophy.

On the other hand, constructivism entails an active process of learning and is generally associated with the work of the Russian psychologist, Lev Vygotsky. Moore (2012:18–19) summarizes Vygotsky's views on development, instruction and consciousness. Cognitive development is achieved most effectively by elaborating ideas and understandings in discussion with teachers or pedagogical experts and peers. Learners perform and develop better with help than without help, and are given tasks that will test what is developing in them rather than what has already developed (the notion of stretching not just "able" students, but those who may be perceived as under-achieving in comparison with any accepted developmental or positional norm). Learners aim to develop "conscious mastery" over what they have learned rather than merely being able to recite facts which may have little meaning for them. The development of such expertise is not subject-specific, and once acquired becomes a tool through which all learning is facilitated and enhanced. Student–teacher relations therefore are dialogic rather than monologic, involve collaborative learning, both with peers and the teacher, recognize learning as an active and interactive process concerned with the provisional nature of the student's knowledge, and emphasize articulation and meta-processes of learning.

## 6.3 LEARNING SETS OR SEQUENCES

From this constructivist perspective and in line with the elements required for a learning theory that we referred to above, it is possible to identify a series of learning sets or sequences. The first of these is *observation*. Here the teacher performs the action that the learner is required to imitate in the classroom, and then later in the context of application. These are stimuli for learning (cf., Bandura, 1977).

The *coaching model* has a series of steps: modelling by the expert; coaching whilst the learner practices; scaffolding where the learner is supported during the initial stages with that support gradually being withdrawn as the learner becomes more proficient; articulation by the learner of that process; reflection on those processes and comparison with the expert's reasons for action; and exploration where the learner undertakes the various activities without support (cf., Collins *et al.*, 1989).

*Goal clarity* is a component of effective learning. To this end, teachers need to provide learners with explicit statements and explanations about the instructional objectives in a lesson or series of lessons. Goal clarity has three learner-focused aspects: explanations about how they are expected to perform the tasks assigned to them; opportunities for them to grasp what is expected of them; and reflections about their capacity as self-directed learners in the completion of the task (cf., Zimmerman and Schunk, 2011; Meece *et al.*, 2006).

*Mentoring* supports the informal transmission of knowledge, social capital or psychosocial resources. It is usually conducted face-to-face and involves a relationship between two people, one of whom is considered to have greater knowledge, wisdom or experience. Five possible mentoring techniques have been identified: (i) supporting the student and even taking part in the same activity and learning side-by-side with the learner; (ii) preparing the student for the future even if they are not ready or able to learn what is being offered to them in the present; (iii) catalyzing learning, provoking a different way of thinking, a change in identity or a re-ordering of values; (iv) showing through personal example; and finally, (v) helping and supporting the learner in reflecting back on their previous learning (cf., Aubrey and Cohen, 1995).

*Peer learning* is defined as learning from and with the learner's peers. The other forms of learning comprise unequal relations between the teacher and the learner. Here the assumption is made that the learning relationship is between equals, and thus a different form of learning is implied. Examples of this type of learning include: affective support—being offered emotional support if learning proves to be difficult, and this is always a better form of support if given by someone who is going through the same learning process; dyadic performance confrontations—learning is provoked by confrontational exchanges between students so that each student can test his or her own theories, ideas and constructs against those held by learners engaged in the same form of learning; pair-problem-solving—here learning is enabled through cooperation between two learners of roughly equal standing, so that in a problem-solving exercise, better solutions are forthcoming because there are two problem-solvers rather than one; reciprocal peer tutoring—non-expert tutoring between equals has the advantage of each person being able to make their own evaluation of the advice being offered unencumbered by status or hierarchy; and scripted cooperative dyads—here peer engagement is focused on the joint production of a script, artefact, performance or text with the result that alternative and new interpretations/readings are forthcoming (cf., Falchikov, 2001).

A *simulation* is a reproduction of an event or activity, conducted outside the environment where that event or activity usually takes place. Simulations can be produced through computer games, role-plays, scenarios, presentations and affective and conceptual modelling. The purpose of this learning process is to simulate a real event, and this is to allow the person or persons taking part in that simulation to explore it, to experiment within it, to understand the process, to begin the process of internalization, to experience, albeit in a limited way, the emotions and feelings that would normally accompany the experience in real-life, and fundamentally, to allow learning to take place through trial and error by making mistakes in safe situations, which do not have the consequences they would have in real-life situations.

With *instruction*, the teacher needs to: gain the attention of the group of learners; inform the learners of the objectives of the learning exercise (i.e., what is intended to be learnt); stimulate recall of prior learning amongst the group of learners, so that the new information is related productively to previous and current learning; present content to the student; implement appropriate scaffolding processes; stimulate a performance by the student; provide feedback to the student which is a comment on the student's performance and allows corrective action to take place; and lastly evaluate the corrected performance (cf., Gagne, 1985).

*Concept-formation* focuses on the re-forming of conceptual schema that the learner has about the world and, in the particular case here, about those conceptual matters relating to schools, classrooms and teaching-learning processes. Learning is complex and potentially rich and rewarding, where the student is presented with a mass of information, ideas, schema, opinions from a number of different sources (e.g., books, articles, lectures, seminars, emails, e-seminars, personal communications and so on). What the learner does is shape this mass of information, and this shaping can take a number of different forms: partial shaping, complete shaping, discarding with no replacement, confusion, on-going, going backwards and forwards and so on.

The Learning Cycle, developed by David Kolb (1984), is based on a belief that deep learning (learning for real comprehension) comes from a sequence of experience, reflection, abstraction, and active testing. *Reflection* is a form of evaluative thinking. It is applied to ideas for which there is no obvious solution, and is largely based on the further processing of knowledge and understanding, and possibly emotions, that we already possess. It is thus a second-order internal activity, which can in certain circumstances be transformed into a learning strategy.

*Meta-cognition* refers to learners' awareness of their own knowledge and their ability to understand, control, and manipulate their own cognitive processes. However, most meta-cognitive processes can be classified within the following categories (Harris & Graham, 1992). The first is meta-memory. This refers to the learners' awareness of and knowledge about their own memory systems and strategies for using their memories effectively. The second is meta-comprehension. This term refers to the learners' ability to monitor the degree to which they understand information being communicated to them, to recognize failures to comprehend, and to employ repair strategies when failures are identified. The third is self-regulation. This term refers to the learners' ability to make adjustments in their own learning processes in response to their perception of feedback regarding their current state of learning.

Learners find out for themselves rather than being given answers to problems; this is a *problem-solving pedagogy.* They are required to engage in a series of interrogative processes with regards to texts, people and objects in the environment, and come up with solutions to problems. They are also required to use the skills of information retrieval, information synthesis and analysis, and knowledge organization. Learners may come up with inadequate, incorrect and faulty syntheses and analyses. However, this is acceptable because the learning resides in the process rather than in the end-product. Problem-solving learning involves learners in judging their own work against a curriculum standard and engaging in meta-processes of learning (i.e., an understanding about processes of one's own learning; the development of learning pathways; the utilization of formative assessment processes; the development of personal learning strategies; and the internalization of the curriculum).

Finally, there is *practice* (which is the act of rehearsing behaviour over and over again, or engaging in an activity again and again). This reinforces, enhances and deepens the learning associated with the behaviour or activity.

These twelve sets or sequences (observation, coaching, goal clarity, mentoring, peer learning, simulation, instruction, concept-formation, reflection, meta-cognition, problem-solving, and practice) are general modes of learning and need to be understood as they are used with and through the new digital technologies. However, before we do this, we need to reflect on the idea of independent or self-regulated learning.

## 6.4 INDEPENDENT LEARNING

There are a number of different terms that are used to describe independent learning, with perhaps the most common being "self-regulated learning". All these different terms have common features: learners have a meta-cognitive understanding of how they are learning; they are motivated to take responsibility for their learning; and they monitor and structure their own learning experiences. As is the case with many terms commonly used in higher education learning, "independent learning" can mean different things to different people, in different disciplines and in different cultures. Foster (1972: ii), for example, defines independent learning/study in the following way: "independent study is a process, a method and a philosophy of education: in which a student acquires knowledge by his or her own efforts and develops the ability for inquiry and critical evaluation; it includes freedom of choice in determining those objectives, within the limits of a given project or programme and with the aid of a faculty adviser; it requires freedom of process to carry out the objectives; and it places increased educational responsibility on the student for the achieving of objectives and for the value of the goals". This clearly places responsibility for learning on the student, aided by the teaching staff and defined by the limits and objectives of the programme, and more importantly, by the limitations built into the teaching and learning approaches, including the use of digital technologies.

The extent to which independent learning is culturally situated is of some concern. Adult learning theory (e.g., Freire, 1972; Knowles, 1990; and Mezirow, 1991, are some of the most influential proponents and developers) has been criticized for a lack of sensitivity to diversity, cultural inviolability and false universalism. Recognizing this and using Foster's (1972) definition of independent learning, independent learning can be seen quite broadly to encompass a variety of situations and contexts where students are interpreting and absorbing new knowledge and skills independently from those around them. Seen in this light, independent learning does not need to be understood as being isolated, but can also take place within a community of learners, even in a virtual environment, and where those other people are not literally present.

Tools for independent learning include: e-portfolios (collections of multimedia including texts, images, audios, blogs); peer-mentoring schemes; study skills sessions (goal setting, time management, working to deadlines, self-appraisal, reading); and on-going training in using online information. The skills and knowledge of effectively using online information are important for independent learning.

## 6.5 DIGITAL TEACHING AND LEARNING APPROACHES

Digital technologies have the potentiality to change the learning experience in a number of very distinct ways. These include: portability, flexibility, transferability, inter-changeability, enhanced student autonomy, the development of a hypertextual model of text production, recording and accessing meta-cognitive progress, storage and retrieval capabilities, enhanced peer-learning opportunities, and more comprehensive referencing facilities. All of these have the capacity to change the learning process, so that knowledge development is not only achieved in more efficient ways but is qualitatively changed. Its dimensions, its uses, its effects and its consequences are now different from what they were before. What do we mean by all these different processes?

Previously, we suggested that a learning environment, virtual or otherwise, has a number of distinctive features: a determination of the circumstances in which learning can take place in the specific environment; a set of resources and technologies to allow that learning to take place; a particular type of relationship between teacher and learner to effect that learning; a theory of learning, that is, an account of how the learning (expressed as a knowledge set, skill or disposition/inclination) can be assimilated; and a further account of how the learning taking place in a particular set of circumstances (for example, in an institution of higher education, with a set of learners, in a particular way, with a particular theory of learning underpinning it, and so forth), can transfer to environments in other places and times. What this means is that there is a series of elements which distinguish one type of learning environment from another, so a face-to-face learning environment (let us call it $L_a$) can be distinguished from a virtual learning environment (let us call it $L_b$). Some of these features are: a specific type of pedagogic arrangement; a type of relation between the different knowledge domains; a focus on or orientation towards knowledge or skill; a measure of progression or pacing in the learning environment; a type of relation between teacher and taught, and between types of learners; a set of spatial relations, and a set of temporal relations; and finally, a particular set of criteria for evaluating that learning.

Portability refers to the capacity of the learner to choose where he or she studies so they are not restricted, as they are in traditional forms of face-to-face learning, by having to be in one place, and incidentally in a particular time-moment. Access to the learning environment is gained through a computer terminal, which can be carried around from place to place. Learning in a virtual learning environment allows a measure of flexibility, denied to those studying in traditional environments. This flexibility means that students have some control over when they study, where they study, with whom they study, for how long they study, at what times in their lives they study, and what they study. Although traditional learning environments try to build in flexible routes and pathways through the programme of learning, they are clumsy artefacts compared with a well-constructed virtual learning environment (see Figure 6.1 over page, in which a traditional face-to-face learning environment is portrayed).

Transferability is another feature of virtual learning environments. They allow the student, as well as the teacher, to develop tasks beyond the physical environment of the classroom, widening access to education. More importantly, they have the capacity to extend the range of pedagogic resources that are available in the learning setting, albeit that many of these resources are virtual. Another feature of a virtual learning environment is its capacity for inter-changeability and consequently, its ability to respond to changing circumstances and individual needs. So personalized programmes of learning can be more easily sustained in a virtual learning environment, than in a traditional face-to-face setting, and units and elements of the programme can be moved around to suit particular needs, thus creating new relations and connections between them.

*Figure 6.1 Oil on canvas by Krzyszt of Lubieniecki / 1717. "School-teacher".*

Virtual learning environments allow a measure of student autonomy that even the best of traditional learning programmes find difficult to replicate. This is because, in theory at least, virtual learning environments have the capacity to reconfigure the relationship between learner and stimulus. Instead of a form of textual production that privileges the writer over the reader—or in the case that we are considering here—the teacher over the learner, what we have now is the possibility, though it is rarely exploited, of this relationship becoming a much more equal one. That is, the reader and the writer, or the teacher and the learner, are now co-producers of texts, including learning texts or products. This new hypertextual model of representation has profound implications for the types of learning that can now be used and has been occasioned by the invention and large-scale adoption of digital technologies.

Another advantage of the use of digital media is that online lectures become relatively easy to create and deliver, offering flexibility for teachers and students, allowing them to participate at their own pace and in line with their own schedules. An interesting example is the Khan Academy[4] learning programme. This programme has successfully produced more than 3,000 videos, seen monthly by almost 4 million students, who have performed more than 2 million exercises in relation to them each day. There is a similar Brazilian initiative with great potential (*Veduca*, which we refer to in Chapter 7), and this initiative was to make the best higher education courses from Brazil and the rest of the world available to everybody. So far, almost 5,000 classes have been made available, with more than 200 courses and almost 100,000 exhibitions. Another example is the biochemist programme at Stanford University (Prober and Heat, 2012), which was recently redesigned following this model. Instead of a standard lecture-based format, the instructors provide short online presentations, allowing class time to be used for interactive discussions.

Two further elements of virtual learning environments are: recording and accessing meta-cognitive progress, and storage and retrieval facilities. We have suggested in this chapter that independent learning approaches have one cardinal advantage: they are self-regulated learning approaches. These reflexive and reflective elements are enhanced by the capacity of the system to store (in a retrievable form) previous traces of learning (i.e., oral and written contributions to virtual conferences, memos and analytical notes, chronologies of actions and accounts of working processes for supplying solutions to problems that were eventually solved). The human memory is not an adequate substitute for electronic storage and retrieval processes. Finally, virtual learning environments and the World Wide Web are able to store a wider range of resources (e.g., texts, illustrations, diagrams, traces of civilization), and thus have a more comprehensive library to be accessed by the learner. These elements of virtual learning environments (portability, flexibility, transferability, interchangeability, enhanced student autonomy, the development of a hypertextual model of text production, recording and accessing meta-cognitive progress, storage and retrieval capabilities, enhanced peer-learning opportunities, and more comprehensive referencing facilities), provide opportunities for more effective, efficient and productive learning to take place. Although it is important not to treat traditional face-to-face and digital learning as bipolar or binary oppositional, it certainly has to be acknowledged that digital learning environments allow some forms of learning denied to those operating in traditional environments.

## 6.6 LEARNING SKILLS

In summary, there are skills such as studying in advance, work-based learning, using information technology, interpersonal capacities, and enterprise incubator participation, that can be learned and applied in self-directed or independent learning. The principal skills and attributes required for independent learning can be summarized as: cognitive, metacognitive, motivational, persistence, pedagogic, and preparatory. *Cognitive* skills include those related to memory, attention and problem-solving. Students need to have reached a certain level of cognitive development, such as being able to decode basic information as they embark on independent learning, and their teachers must be able to promote this cognitive development to sustain independent learning. The second element is *metacognitive*. As we suggested above, this comprises three processes: meta-memorization, meta-comprehension, and most importantly, self-regulation. This refers to the learners' ability to make adjustments in their own learning processes in response to their perception of feedback regarding their current state of learning.

The third element relates to the *motivational* capacity of the learner. This is directly associated with increased independent learning and can also be an outcome of it. In other words, in order to benefit fully from a programme of independent learning, the learner has to be motivated to do so. In addition, success on the programme is likely to further motivate the student to do well on other elements of the programme. The fourth element is *persistence*, where the learner does not give up even after encountering a series of difficulties. The fifth element is *pedagogic*. This refers to the facilitative role played by the teacher and the substituting of didactic learning approaches for auto-directed learning strategies. Finally, there is the notion of *preparation* and the need for the student to prepare him or herself before embarking on digital programmes of study. In the next chapter, we will provide some examples of independent and transformatory learning approaches as they are being enacted in Brazil.

## NOTES

1. As seen at: http://thinkexist.com/quotation/thinking-is-like-loving-or-dying-each-of-us-must/1084687.html. Accessed August, 2012.

2. As seen at: http://ocw.mit.edu/index.htm/. Accessed May 2013.
3. Young, J.R. Providers of free MOOCs now charge employers for access to student data, *Chronicle of Higher Education* (4 December), 2012. As seen at: http://chronicle.com/article/providers-of-free-MOOCs-Now/136117/. Accessed May, 2013.
4. CDIO, Conceiving, Designing, Implementing and Operating Real-world Systems and Products, 2012. Available at: http://www.cdio.org. Accessed August 2012.

# CHAPTER 7

# Case Studies in Brazil

*We need permanently to aspire to something, which, once achieved, will lead us to think to the next ambition.*
**(Carlos Drummond de Andrade, 1990)**

In this chapter, we engage with the problems and processes of education for innovation. In doing this, we have selected a number of case studies that we feel are examples of successful innovation practices. These case studies have provided better educational experiences for students, and allowed those students to make productive connections between innovation and education. This, we suggest, has had the effect of increasing sustainable economic growth across the regions of Brazil, resulting in a better quality of life for these regional populations. Our cases in Brazil also include successful models of implementation, and these cases are: the Digital Educational Project in Piraí-RJ; the C.E.S. A.R. and the 3Es: Engineering, Education and Entrepreneurship; the Veduca Educational Experiment; the Start-up Neoprospecta; and the Lemann Centre for Educational Entrepreneurship and Innovation.

There are four dimensions to policy implementation: (i) making sure that the reform programme is comprehensive, satisfactory and serviceable; (ii) understanding how the implementation site is currently constructed; (iii) specifying how the current implementation site will need to be changed to accommodate the new initiative; and (iv) determining how this new initiative can be institutionalized so that it functions effectively over time. We might want to call these four dimensions: *the new programme structure*; *implementation sites*; *implementation capacity*; and *institutionalization and sustainability processes*.

The first element refers to the internal relations of the new practice which is to be transferred to a new setting (e.g., the new programme structure). A model of a new productive practice (or reform) has a number of characteristics. It has a set of elements arranged in a logically coherent way (e.g., an arrangement of resources, functions and roles for people in the system, and accountability relationships). It has a causal narrative (e.g., the productive practice is such that *a* leads to *b*; or the implementation of $a$ in ideal circumstances leads to $b_1$, $b_2$, $b_3$ and so on). And there is a rationale (ethical, practical and consequential) for the productive practice and for its implementation. In order to fully develop this first element, producers, educational reformers, and policy-implementers need to provide satisfactory answers to the following questions: What is the problem that needs a solution? Why is the solution appropriate? What are the characteristics of the ideal model (e.g., identification of elements, relations between these elements, a causal narrative and possible effects)? And why is the ideal model appropriate?

The second element of our change model comprises giving an account of how the current system, into which the new productive practice is to be implemented, works. This means that the investigator/implementer needs to identify and evaluate: how the system currently works; current arrangements of people and resources; current allocations of people to functions and roles; and current outputs from the system. In order to fully develop this second element, producers, educational reformers, and policy-implementers need to provide satisfactory answers to the following questions: Which elements of the system relating to the chosen productive practice (e.g., the reform) are satisfactory and which are unsatisfactory? Why are they satisfactory or why are they unsatisfactory? Which arrangements of people and resources in relation to the chosen productive practice (e.g., the reform) are satisfactory and which are unsatisfactory? Why are they satisfactory or why are they unsatisfactory? Which allocations of people to functions and roles in relation to the chosen productive practice (e.g., the reform) are satisfactory and which are unsatisfactory? Why are they satisfactory or why are they unsatisfactory? Which outputs from the current system are satisfactory or unsatisfactory? And why are they satisfactory or unsatisfactory?

The third element refers to the new site of practice or the implementation site. In the first instance an account needs to be provided, which specifies: the arrangements of resources in the new productive practice; likely changes to the arrangement of resources as a result of implementing the productive practice; possible arrangements of people to functions and roles in the new productive practice; likely changes to allocations of people to functions and roles as a result of implementing the productive practice; the desired rate of change; the intended effects of implementing the productive practice (e.g., the planned consequences); possible unintended effects of implementing the productive practice—these are speculations about what might happen and this refers to unplanned effects; and strategies for minimizing unintended effects if they occur.

Capacity development, central to the implementation of the productive practice, is a learning process. This means that there is a need to specify: the circumstances in which learning can take place in the specific learning environment; the resources and technologies needed to allow that learning to take place; the type of relationship between teacher and student, and student and student, to effect that learning; a theory of learning—for example, how that construct (e.g., knowledge set, skill or disposition) can be assimilated; a theory of transfer held by the teacher; that is, how can the learning that has taken place in a particular set of circumstances (e.g., a classroom in a university, with a set of students in a particular way, with a particular theory of learning underpinning it, and so forth) transfer to other environments in other places and times; an appropriate fit between learning outcomes *and* learning approaches; appropriate theory-to-practice, practice-to-theory, and practice-to-theory-to-practice, relations in the learning sequence. There is also a need to put in place appropriate arrangements of resources to allow that capacity to be realized. Capacity also needs to relate appropriately to new arrangements and amounts of resources, and to new allocations of persons to functions and roles. The reason for this is that developing and realizing human capacity has two elements: what is learnt (e.g., knowledge sets, skills and dispositions); and, just as importantly, arrangements of resources that allow such knowledge sets, skills and dispositions to be realized.

The fourth and final stage is the institutionalizing and sustainability process. It is important, in the first instance, to formatively evaluate the implementation of the productive practice to allow continuous improvement to the initiative. Evaluative practices can be regarded as formative, if evidence is gathered relating to the programme of activity being evaluated; that evidence is *elicited*, *interpreted*, and *used* by the practitioner, the policy-maker or an interested party. Such evidence is used by them with the specific intention of deciding on the subsequent steps in the development of the productive practice. The productive practice is in a constant state of change and development. The longevity and sustainability of the new productive practice *in situ*, and as it is being implemented, depends on: resource arrangements; allocations of particular people to positions of responsibility; particular roles and arrangements of power and authority; and the capacity of key people in the system, policy discourses and new policies.

In order to fully develop this final element, producers, educational reformers, and policy-implementers need to provide satisfactory answers to the following questions: What evaluative systems are in place for monitoring the progress of the reform? What resource arrangements are in place for ensuring longevity and sustainability to the reform? What allocations of people to positions of responsibility are in place for providing longevity and sustainability to the reform? What arrangements of power and authority are in place for ensuring longevity and sustainability to the reform? What capacities do people in the system have for ensuring longevity and sustainability to the reform? What capacities are there within the system for adapting to changes in resource allocations? And what capacities are there within the system for adapting to changes in policy discourses and new policies?

The five cases we are focusing on here in Brazil are all successful examples of initiatives that continue to have positive benefits for the communities which sustain them. Brazil is a land of contrasts, where only the privileged few have access to universities, with the result that only 11% of the population of working-age has a higher education degree. As a consequence, graduates earn, on average, two and a half times as much as those without a first degree but who finished secondary education, and around five times as much as the majority who didn't graduate from secondary schools. The difference between university graduates and non-graduates is higher than all other OECD members. Although there have been recent changes to the profile of students, especially with regards to non-fee paying public (state-operated and funded) universities, they are predominantly white and affluent compared with the rest of the population and much more likely to have been educated privately.

Recent initiatives such as the ProUni Programme[1], which emanated from the Federal Government's offer to private universities to allow tax breaks in return for providing around a tenth of their places free or at a discount to students coming from families on modest incomes, have helped to change the Brazilian educational scene.

This programme has benefitted more than 1 million students since 2005. Another half million students per year are receiving low-interest loans, which is boosting demand and helping to raise standards. Such considerations are important in understanding recent social changes in Brazil, where a new middle class is contributing to reforming the system and entrepreneurship is becoming of increasing importance.

## 7.1 THE DIGITAL EDUCATIONAL PROJECT IN PIRAÍ-RJ

Piraí, a small city in the state of Rio de Janeiro, Brazil, with a population of around 25,000, launched the Piraí Digital Project in February 2004[2]. The origins of the project are associated with initiatives that started in the late 1990s, when the municipality received a small modernization grant from the Federal Government and part of it was used to build a fixed-wireless IP network to inter-connect government offices. The authorities at that time realized that broadband connectivity could be extended to a larger area at little extra cost. In 2001, the Municipal Government formed an advisory board consisting of representatives from government, the residents' associations, academic and non-profit making organizations, and the business and labour unions to develop the digital project and to manage its evolution.

Little more than a decade after the project started, Piraí is considered to be a pioneer in the Brazilian plan for technology integration, having established a programme that reaches both teachers and students at all grade levels. By providing general digital access much earlier than other much bigger cities in Brazil, and by understanding that e-learning resources can play an integral role in education, Piraí is considered to be a successful example of innovatory practice, even to the extent that the town itself is sometimes known as *Piraí Digital*. The *Piraí Digital* project was designed round a notion of learner independence and teaching approaches that moved away from lecture-based and didactic pedagogies and made more use of digital learning technologies, transformative learning approaches and inclusive practices.

The Piraí Digital Project makes use of a network based on Wi-Fi technology that covers the entire town. The network has 39 digital centres with 145 computers in public buildings. In addition, there are 20 digital centres in schools, with 188 computers serving over 6,000 students, 20 access points in public libraries and other institutional computerized modal points. Each centre has an average of 220 users per day[3]. The network uses free Linux software, and is centrally managed, offering internet access, e-mail, e-government services and e-learning.

As Coelho and Jardim point out[4], this programme is part of two larger policy initiatives, one municipal and the other national. These initiatives share the common desire to use information and communication technologies to address Brazil's unemployment and underemployment by developing educative and upskilling strategies. This is feasible because of an extensive level of stakeholder engagement, involving large segments of the community, and serving all the different types of students living and studying in Piraí.

The local programme coordinators were responsible for facilitating the planning process and making possible effective communication between the municipal offices and the schools. To make this happen, teachers and school administrators cooperated together to develop a pedagogical plan. School committees were formed and they focused on the required pedagogical changes needed to implement the reforms, the required knowledge-sharing strategies and how all this impacted on curriculum reforms. Initially, an experimental pilot was carried out at a single school in Piraí. After the success of the pilot, it was decided to extend the programme to the entire town, and the experiences of the students and teachers in the pilot school were used as a base for designing an implementation strategy for the whole community.

Consideration had to be given to the limited town budget, the lack of previous technological infrastructure in the schools and the relatively poor education provision. However, despite this, the project had a number of areas to build on: the community commitment to integrate technology into the schools, financial and technical support from the state and federal governments, and support from business partners like Intel and other companies. A key element of the implementation strategy was allowing a level of autonomy to school leaders so that they were relatively independent in managing their school's strand in the project. In addition, teachers' and students' views on the project were solicited at all phases of the implementation process. This allowed those teachers who had been trained at an early stage of the project, and were thus early adopters, to pass their experiences onto other teachers at the first stages of the integration process, facilitating e-learning adoption in the classrooms. This experience contributed to the development of exemplars of good practice, allowing the possibility of transfer to other cities and other educational settings.

The use of low-cost networking technologies, combined with open source software, dramatically reduced network costs, allowing Piraí to provide broadband services where traditional fixed-line operators could not justify the investment. A group of universities offering online courses agreed to oversee network implementation, on a no-cost basis. Innovative network management and technology choices allowed Piraí to reduce the project's costs dramatically, and made it possible to finance the project from the municipal budget, with only minor financial aid from the Federal Government.

The success of the technology integration programme in Piraí represented an opportunity to change its perspectives on social and economic sustainable development locally. The project was central to a plan to diversify the local economy and attract new investments, following the privatization of the state-owned power utility. Integrating the ICT needs of the public sector, business and educational institutions was a major objective of the project. The emphasis was on four areas: e-government, education and public access and, additionally, a private company with majority municipal ownership was created to commercialize services to households and businesses.

A series of research projects undertaken into this digital project in Piraí (for example, Teles and Joia, 2012) drew contrasting conclusions. The general conclusion was that digital inclusion in Piraí had had a positive impact on local public administration, the educational sector and the health system. However, they also suggested that there had not been a clear and homogeneous impact on other institutions in the locality.

The local programme formed the basis for a pilot project of the federal programme named *Um Computador por Aluno*[5] (in English this is *One Computer per Pupil*), making the Piraí experience an educational exemplar of good practice in which teachers shifted from didactic to facilitative teaching and learning approaches; students adopted, with various degrees of success, independent learning modes; and digital technologies were successfully integrated into the formal educational process. In terms of evaluation and assessment, the biennial federal educational index IDEB[6] indicator registered significant improvement in pilot school fifth-grade completion rates, improving from 2.4 in 2005 to 4.2 in 2007 and to 4.5 in 2009. In 2011, the rate of 5.2 was obtained for fourth-grade and fifth-grade pupils including all the municipal schools, which would indicate a successful outcome for the project.

## 7.2 C.E.S.A.R. AND THE 3Es: ENGINEERING, EDUCATION AND ENTREPRENEURSHIP

In 1996, enthusiastic teachers from the Computer Science Department of the *Universidade Federal de Pernambuco* established a private institution that created products, services and companies using Information Technology and Communication (ITC) and named it the *Recife Centre for Advanced Studies and Systems*, better known under the Portuguese acronym C.E.S.A.R. (*Centro de Estudos de Sistemas Avançados de Recife*)[7]. C.E.S.A.R. has three elements: Engineering, Education and Entrepreneurship, and is one of the few self-sustaining institutions in the world to conduct all of these activities simultaneously.

The first move to establish C.E.S.A.R. was in 1992, when an incubator called BEAT was created. The results were not completely satisfactory but the experience gained was fruitful. In 1997, C.E.S.A.R. developed a different strategy in which the first call for action had to come from the satellite companies, in contrast to the previous strategy, and it had to be a response to a specific problem identified by the client itself. About 10 years ago, C.E.S.A.R. moved to a different area of Recife, joining the newly created cluster Porto Digital, an ITC environment of entrepreneurship, innovation and business. Today, C.E.S.A.R. is part of Porto Digital, which has become one of the most important Brazilian technological centres—a base for over 200 companies housed in downtown Recife. The enterprise was a part of a very interesting project of urban renewal in the previously depressed area of *Bairro do Recife* Island, capital of the State of Pernambuco in the Brazilian northeast. Its presence was essential to help consolidate this area as a business centre by attracting a number of related companies. C.E.S.A.R. headquarters is currently proudly housed in an early twentieth century 2.090 m$^2$ renovated warehouse in downtown Recife. It has a total space of about 2.783 m$^2$, with more than 430 workstations, as well as a library, auditorium, meeting rooms, training rooms, production areas and several laboratories[7].

The State of Pernambuco was convinced of the need to invest in the infrastructure for an innovation cluster and the Federal and Municipal governments have also supported the project. Porto Digital now comprises 173 entities, 143 of which are companies, and 6,500 ITC professionals, with a resulting annual turnover of more than US$ 400 million. Nowadays, the ITC sector represents around 4% of Pernambuco's GDP and its goal is to reach 10% by 2020[8]. In less than 17 years of existence, C.E.S.A.R., besides transforming Recife by helping to create the Porto Digital, can be considered today as one of the most impactful private initiatives in Brazil. This contribution has been recognized by several awards, twice (in 2004 and 2010) being considered as "the most innovative science and technology institution in Brazil" by FINEP (the Federal Government Financing Agency for Projects and Studies).

C.E.S.A.R. now has more than 400 collaborators whose R&D skills help their clients take their business to another level by creating and implementing innovative solutions based on information technology. From the beginning, the developed products and services had to cover the entire innovation process, from idea to project execution, for the telecommunications, electronics, commercial automation, finance, media, energy, health, and agro-business industries. The C.E.S.A.R. innovation process phases are as follows: firstly, research to develop a profile of a specific public and identify opportunities for innovation. As techniques, it has a context diagnostic, a trend follow up, and a definition of initial strategy. Secondly, an ideational phase, associated with the brainstorming of solutions based on collected data, followed by a joint selection of proposals based on legitimacy criteria with users and clients. At this phase, the techniques it uses are: ethnography, laboratory focus groups, interviews, and statistical methods. The third phase is prototyping, a phase related to the production of design alternatives (artefacts or experiences) via prototyping in increasing levels of accuracy, from paper prototypes to full working models. The techniques it uses are: planning, definitions of roadmaps from the business case, and the development of prototypes. The final phase, evaluation, includes prototype execution and field testing to anticipate problems and to fit the artefact or experience to a user's needs. In addition, and as associated techniques for this phase, use is made of: profile creation, risk surveys, work schedule preparation, resources surveys, user recruiting, task planning, a definition of test procedures, and a results analysis process.

Among C.E.S.A.R. clients are companies like Motorola, Samsung, Vivo, Oi, Positivo, Dell, Visanet, Bematech, Bradesco, Unibanco, Banco Central do Brasil, Siemens, Philips, CHESF and the Federal Water Board (ANA). These enterprises have contracted C.E.S.A.R. services to perform studies, prototype and develop solutions for their businesses. C.E.S.A.R.'s partnership with multinational corporations has provided a number of unique experiences. Some of these initiatives are[7]: assisting Motorola in the creation of that company's Brazil Test Centre for verification and validation of cell phone software sold worldwide; participation in the Instinct Project with the European Community for the development of Digital TV technologies; a partnership with IBM in the development of solutions at OSGi Alliance, an international consortium for the development of a process that ensures interoperability of applications and services based on its integration platform; and a partnership with Intel, Popcatcher, AW-G and Sensaura for the development of technology to capture songs in real time with the use of artificial intelligence.

To illustrate, one, among many, success histories of companies created by the project, there is the Silicon Reef case[9]. Although emanating from C.E.S.A.R., Silicon Reef was prepared to leave and move to independent facilities within Porto Digital, after completing the C.E.S.A.R. cycle: starting as a project, then, became formally incorporated, and finally fully independent. This particular green company specializes in low-power integrated circuits producing chips to treat the energy coming from solar panels and optimizing them. Its potential clients are solar panels' manufacturers, as well as any companies whose products include such panels. In 2008, the enterprise initially received public funding, making it possible to hire a team, and one year later its business model won the Challenge Brazil Premium.

Nowadays, although fully integrated with the State and local companies, C.E.S.A.R. does not depend for its health directly on these clients, as 98% of its turnover does not come from Pernambuco. As a consequence, it has established commercial offices in other regions, like São Paulo, Curitiba and other cities, creating the conditions to identify problems on behalf of their clients and address them across

Brazil. With regard to providing a stimulus for entrepreneurship, the company named C.E.S.A.R. PAR was recently created to manage its work in the companies it had created so far and to provide venture capital. These can take different forms: C.E.S.A.R. can choose to become the main stakeholder or look for external venture capital. There is also a plan to launch again its Garage project which had been suspended in 2009 due to the international financial crisis. Part of the resources coming from the developed projects for its clients is invested in education via C.E.S.A.R. EDU[10]. There are 20 Computer Science undergraduate programs and six postgraduate ones that contribute to the education of professionals in ICT, because this department was created with the mission of developing world class ICT professionals. C.E.S.A.R. EDU's faculty are professionals with a broad experience of working with domestic and international companies providing the perfect complement to academia, working hand in hand with the corporate world for the creation of innovative solutions by innovative professionals.

## 7.3 THE VEDUCA EDUCATIONAL EXPERIMENT

Veduca is a Brazilian company recently founded by four young entrepreneurs, three with an engineering and one with a computer science background, with its main purpose being to democratize high quality education in Brazil via video-lectures in Portuguese from world-class universities[11]. Since its launch on 1 March 2012, they have developed targets and strategies based on the assumption that the education system in Brazil is in a critical state, with deficiencies in access and quality. For instance, although the total number of students enrolled in higher education (6.7 million[12]) has increased in the last decade at a rate (178%) that is higher than other Organization for Economic Co-operation and Development (OECD) countries[13], the percentage of the population with completed tertiary level qualifications in Brazil is still less than 10%. This is extremely low compared with an average of around 30% in OECD countries.

The use of digital technologies has the possibility of speeding up the process of meeting demand from an accelerating and growing economy. Nevertheless, the Brazilian map of online education, as identified by Veduca's founders, shows that activity in this area is still at a basic level and mainly focused on preparatory education, leaving a gap in provision at higher education and academic levels. Any online education that exists uses basic rather than sophisticated technologies. In general, most of the currently available material has low quality control and loose unrelated contents. Even if a decision was made to borrow academic contents from international websites, this is a flawed strategy, because only about 2% of the general population in Brazil speaks English, making it impossible for the large majority of Brazilian students to understand and make efficient use of such contents. However, there is evidence that online learners are expanding their reach and influence in Brazil and the use of digital technologies in other areas such as electronic banking, elections, etc., has been successfully achieved. Recent data[14] shows that there are more than 60 million online users for educational purposes and almost 10 million students on online courses.

The extent and quality of distance education in Brazil is commented upon in the CensoEAD.BR[15], an analytic report of distance learning in Brazil promoted by the Brazilian Association for Distance Education (ABED, in Portuguese: *Associação Brasileira de Educação a Distância*). In 2011, in higher education institutions adopting distance learning processes, 780,000 enrolments were registered, mostly belonging to private institutions, 60.5% of which were profit-led and 14.5% were non-profit businesses. Enrolments in maintained and federal and state government institutions accounted for 15% of the total, 8% in federal and 7% in state schools. In accordance with the census, major obstacles were found to be: the cost of technical solutions (23%), followed by the production cost of courses (17%) and information technology support for clients (14%). Veduca aims to provide the necessary stimulus to the workforce in this area of Brazil.

Veduca was founded with the clear purpose of becoming the biggest video-lecture digital website in Brazil, aiming to impact up on almost 25 million users (which corresponds to around 16% of the total Brazilian population) with high quality education material, most of which is made available in Portuguese. This user target has four elements: 4,000,000 pre-higher education students; 6,700,000 higher education students; 231,000 higher education teachers; and 14,400,000 professionals up to the age of fifty with higher education degrees. Particularly in relation to executive education, and in general associated with Master's in Business Administration (MBA) programmes, the education programme is designed to meet growing demand and keep apace with the expanding economy. Veduca has delivered 5,040 video-lectures from top universities around the world, including very prestigious institutions such as: Berkeley, Columbia, Harvard, Michigan, MIT, NYU, Princeton, Stanford, UCLA, UNSW and Yale. As a result, after only 11 months of existence, and having no paid advertising and being helped by free media exposure in key Brazilian outlets, more than 1.4 million visits have been registered, and also Veduca appears today as a popular result in Google's organic searches for available courses in Portuguese in practically all knowledge fields.

Veduca's curriculum is comprehensive and freely accessed. There are no registration processes, users are encouraged to comment on what is provided, rate the particular lectures and create favourite playlists. Through a proprietary algorithm, using *subs-search*, the learners, by defining the key word, can find lectures and videos positioned at the moment of their last use. Through collaborative subtitling, any user can translate the video-lectures into Portuguese. Another proprietary algorithm *ContentSense* connects the current news agenda, via *KeyNews*, with appropriate lectures and specific content. The principal growth strategy for Veduca is to make the company synonymous with high quality learning through open access, multi-lingual and comprehensive curricular contents.

## 7.4 START-UP NEOPROSPECTA

Entrepreneurship education is an important exemplar of innovatory practice. A number of teaching and learning approaches for entrepreneurship have been suggested: the use of the classics as a form of linguistic learning; action learning; new venture simulations; technology-based simulations; the development of real enterprises; skills-based courses; video role-playing; experiential learning, reflective learning, and mentoring. We have discussed some of these already (see Chapter 6), although as general pedagogic mechanisms rather than specific approaches for entrepreneurship education. There are also debates in the teaching and learning literature as to whether entrepreneurship can be taught or is formed through experience; whether theory plays a significant part in learning or whether it is essentially a practical subject; and what are the appropriate sites of learning (e.g., the workplace or the academy or a combination of the two).

Those elements in general, at least from the Brazilian perspective, have been increasingly associated with the presence of enterprise incubator initiatives in the academic environment. Those incubators have been responsible for part of the student academic training and in many cases are integrated into the official curriculum. They use two specific teaching and learning methods that we identified above: the creation of new venture simulations and the development of real enterprises, which operate in every way as established businesses, but in addition provide learning-on-the-job experiences for potential entrepreneurs or entrepreneurial students.

Neoprospecta[16] is a biotech start-up with a focus on the discovery and development of enzymes from the Brazilian biodiversity. By using high-throughput genomics and bioinformatics, the mission is to speed up the process of new gene finding, exploring the opportunities associated with millions of new enzymes waiting to be discovered in the vast Brazilian biodiversity. It constitutes a very interesting example of a student initiative closely associated with independent learning; in this case it helps to bridge the gap between the knowledge produced at universities and the market. Besides providing continuous support and information to the customers interested in genomic services, Neoprospecta (see Figure 7.1) is also committed to the development of innovative services and products, having a largely untouched rich source of new genetic information.

In addition to their undergraduate and graduate courses, Neoprospecta have established an enterprise that offers two different state of the art services: molecule bio prospecting and an environmental diagnostic, with a

Figure 7.1 Neoprospecta logo[25].

huge potential to meet demand, and indeed to create new demand. They have done this in a rational and sustainable way, creating conditions for innovative projects for the future. The bio-prospecting service specializes in the discovery, identification and systematic analysis of molecular information derived from Brazilian biodiversity, with subsequent commercialization through an online platform, making use of the intellectual property associated with molecule bio-prospecting. In this way, it establishes a rational model and allows a non-destructive exploitation of biodiversity. The environmental diagnostic service specializes in identifying and monitoring biological diversity in this particular area of analysis. This service can be applied, for instance, to monitor the emission of waste and effluents into the environment by industrial plants, and in food supply chains, to ensure the quality of the used inputs and guarantee the absence of contamination in various stages of production. This same service can also be used in hospitals and healthcare facilities, aiming to identify potential sources of infection, through the analysis of micro-organisms present in pathological equipment, facilities, clothing, and other environments, thus allowing preventative actions on the part of hospital managers, with consequent reductions in cases of nosocomial infections.

Neoprospecta won the 2010 Santander Entrepreneurship Award in the Biotechnology and Health category. The prize was a recognition for the effort and pioneering of the Neoprospecta team in the construction of an innovative biotechnology company in Brazil. Neoprospecta also became the winner of the *II Premio Iberoamericano a la Innovación y el Emprendimiento* 2011 (II Ibero-American Award for Innovation and Entrepreneurship), an international prize that recognizes innovative projects from Ibero-America. Neoprospecta offered for this award a project for a large-scale metagenomic database of the Brazilian microbiological biodiversity. The award was presented at the *XXI Cumbre Iberoamericana de Jefes de Estado y de Gobierno* (Ibero-American Summit) in Assunción, Paraguay. In addition, Neoprospecta was recently selected as one of the few companies participating at the 12th Seed Forum 2012 promoted by Finep (the Federal Government Financing Agency for Projects and Studies).

Neoprospecta has developed an original custom-built metagenomic bio-prospecting methodology, through the use of next-generation DNA sequencing and large scale bio-informatics and computational biology. The start-up is able to scrutinize a large number of environmental samples for genes and proteins that can lead to new pharmaceutical and bio-technological products. Metagenomics is a new and tested technology already in use to identify previously unknown genetic technologies, mainly uncultivable micro organisms. Additionally, the enterprise has a trained team in intellectual property management and innovative and genetics-related Brazilian law, ready to help with any questions regarding the legal aspects of bio prospecting. In summary, Neoprospecta is a contract research company, specialized in bio-prospecting of new enzymes, peptides and other proteins.

With respect to the environmental monitoring service, this can be applied to many human activities that have the potential to alter the environment, providing a quantitative and qualitative evaluation of biological diversity present in the monitored environment, over a certain period of time. Several businesses avail themselves both of the service and diagnostic monitoring facility such as industrial plants, buildings, dams, oil rigs, construction, and mining. Enzymes are used in a broad range of industries, like pharmaceutical, biotechnology, fine chemistry, cosmetics, paper, hygiene and sanitation, food and drinks, petro chemistry and bio fuels. The market is very dynamic, highly innovative and open to entrepreneurship. The market is expanding, for example, the market for enzymes is estimated at $3.4 billion (BBC Research—Market Forecast[17]) and the market for anti-cancer molecules derived from marine animals at more than $1 billion, according to a United Nations study. The molecular diagnostic market, in the United States alone is estimated at $2.9 billion, with a projected annual growth of 15% by 2015 (The Future of Molecular Diagnostics, 2010)[18]. It is expected that this market will continue to expand due to the importance of changes relating to the green economy. This trend is derived from the replacement of traditional chemical components in processes and products by enzymes, which are molecules inherently biodegradable and do not produce toxic residues. Similarly, enzymes are generally more efficient in catalysis processes and, as new enzymes are discovered and developed, this will open up new markets.

The financial sustainability of Neoprospecta is guaranteed by the royalties coming from licensing patents associated with the discovery and development of new enzymes and also from the funds from the selling of intellectual property. After one year of activity, Neoprospecta has sequenced and analysed more than 300 billion of DNA base pairs and accumulated experience on the development of proprietary technology for metagenomic diagnostics, besides having established several partnerships with other companies, hospitals and academic institutions. What this suggests is that enterprise development can be characterised in part by the establishment of a broad national and international network by consolidating contacts in industry and academia.

Nowadays, Neoprospecta has two immediate concerns. The first is how to find enzymes on a large scale. The second is how to commercialize and adapt the enzymes. With regard to the first, it implies a need to develop bio-prospect in inhospitable biomes and, after the discovery, they can be further enhanced through protein design and directed evolution. With regard to the second, it has been suggested that a marketplace is developed, which is a web-based system associated with the commercialization of molecular intellectual property. The market will operate with Neoprospecta as the seller of specialized services such as: molecule customization and optimization, directed development, directed bio prospection and legal advice in enzyme related intellectual property. The buyers are those industries which apply for a licensing of molecular intellectual property and they will have access to the market through membership.

The enterprise also offers specialized services like the environmental diagnostic and bio-monitoring, which was developed through Neoprospecta proprietary metagenomics technology. This service provides a complete and cost-effective framework for micro-organism identification and monitoring on a large scale. Another possibility for Neoprospecta is research in areas like genomics, transcriptomics, metagenomics and bioinformatics. In addition, Neoprospecta offers an active specialist service associated with analytical services for the pharmaceutical industry, in a partnership with the *Universidade de Brasilia*. Independent learning technologies have contributed to the success of Neoprospecta[19].

## 7.5 THE LEMANN CENTER FOR EDUCATIONAL ENTREPRENEURSHIP AND INNOVATION

Jorge Paulo Lemann was born in Rio de Janeiro from Swiss immigrant parents. With an estimated net worth of almost US$ 20 billion, he is considered among the 50 richest people in the world by Bloomberg

Billionaire Index[20]. He received his Bachelors degree in Economics in 1961 from Harvard University. In 1971 he founded, together with three partners, the Brazilian investment firm named *Banco Garantia*. During the 1980s, they took control of a Brazilian brewery, resulting in a merger with traditional brands like Brahma, Antártica and Skol, that ultimately became AmBev. In 2004, AmBev merged with Interbrew of Belgium forming InBev, which acquired the American brewer Anheuser-Busch in 2008, thus became one of the world leaders in the brewery market.

In 2008 Lemann founded the *Fundação* Estudar[21], which provides scholarships for Brazilian students. He became a member of the Board of Directors of EndeavorBrazil[22], an international non-profit development organization that finds and supports high-impact entrepreneurs in emerging markets. He also created the Lemann Foundation[23], a non-profit organization with the purpose of training a new generation of policy leaders, technological innovators and entrepreneurs to transform education in Brazil. More recently, in 2012, in a joint initiative with Stanford University School of Education, the Lemann Center for Educational Entrepreneurship and Innovation[24] was launched. The centre aims to significantly improve public education in Brazil in the next decade and to create new educational opportunities inside and outside of the classroom, particularly for Brazil's low-income students. Located within the Stanford University School of Education, the Centre is a ten-year partnership between Stanford and the Lemann Foundation and the activities will predominantly take place on the Stanford campus, with additional exchanges, seminars, and research taking place in Brazil. The Centre also intends to train Brazilian policymakers, technology innovators, and entrepreneurs to improve access and quality in the educational system in Brazil. To achieve this, they aim to attract the best and brightest of Brazil's graduates and professionals from a range of top-ranked fields, including engineering, economics, applied mathematics, and business.

The Centre assumes that a new educational model needs to be developed that not only targets the schools, but the entire ecosystem. This means that to improve student learning, innovation has to come from entrepreneurs, universities, and non-government organizations that are willing to promote teachers, policymakers, creative entrepreneurs, and state-of-the-art technologies. Their purpose would be to concentrate efforts in Brazil to promote improvements to the education system, and the educational ecosystem. In order to increase the participation of the best educators, economists, MBAs, engineers, social scientists, and neuroscientists in the process, the Centre also acts as a training outlet. What underpins this is a belief that academic expertise should be supplemented by a sense of duty, both at international and national levels, a deep commitment to changing the education system in Brazil to improve the quality of life.

To be accepted onto the graduate programme, potential students do not need to have any direct experience of teaching or working in educational institutions. The programmes include training supported by fellowships that are offered annually to those Brazilian students admitted to the School of Education's Master's and doctoral programs and through Stanford's joint MA/MBA program between the Graduate Business School and the School of Education. The intention is that students will be trained to play key roles in Brazilian society in the areas of educational policy, learning design, and educational entrepreneurship. The Centre also intends to host visiting researchers and professionals, especially visiting educational researchers and innovators from Brazil, to attend seminars and to work with Stanford faculty and Lemann Fellowship students. The Centre initially appointed four leading professors: Eric Bettinger, Paulo Blikstein, Martin Carnoy, and David Plank. They work with Lemann Fellows, visiting researchers and professionals, and other Stanford faculty and students to produce and disseminate research on educational policy, technological innovation, measurement, and entrepreneurial projects related to improving Brazilian education. In particular, they are concerned with research related to innovative approaches to educational change.

The Centre is also coordinating an educational think tank in Brazil especially dedicated to the dissemination of advanced and contemporary policy research. The goal of such an initiative is to enhance the impact of academic policy research on education policy debates in Brasilia and the state capitals. This Brazil-based organization will draw on the expertise of Brazilian and other education policy scholars. The Centre will work with the Stanford Teacher Education Programme to train teams of teacher educators in highly effective, innovative methods for preparing high quality teachers in the context of the Brazilian university system. The Centre will focus on developing new approaches to improve learning in Brazilian public schools, especially among low income students, and new learning opportunities for these students inside, and out of, the public school system. This is one manifestation of innovatory educational practice, supported and underpinned by independent, problem-solving and transformatory pedagogies.

## NOTES

1. As seen at: http://prouniportal.mec.gov.br/. Accessed February 2013.
2. As can be seen at: http://www.pirai.rj.gov.br. Accessed February 2013.
3. As can be seen at: http://www.ictregulationtoolkit.org/en/toolkit/notes/PracticeNote/3161. Accessed February 2013.
4. As seen at: http://www.intel.com/content/www/us/en/intel-learning-series/learning-series-brazil-transforms-education-study.html. Accessed February 2013.
5. As can be seen at: http://www.uca.gov.br/institucional/. Accessed February 2013.
6. IDEB-*Índice de Desenvolvimento da Educação Básica* (in English: Basic Education Development Index). As seen at: http://ideb.inep.gov.br/. Accessed February 2013.
7. See http://www.cesar.org.br/english/cesar/organization/
8. See http://thenextweb.com/la/2011/05/22/why-brazils-most-innovative-institution-comes-from-recife/
9. See http://www.siliconreef.com.br/
10. See http://www.cesar.org.br/english/c-e-s-a-r-edu/
11. As seen at: http://www.veduca.com.br/. Accessed February 2013.
12. As seen at: http://portal.inep.gov.br/web/censo-da-educacao-superior. Accessed February 2013.
13. As seen at: http://www.oecd.org/. Accessed February 2013.
14. As seen at: http://www.cetic.br/. Accessed February 2013.
15. CensoEAD.BR: Analytical Report of Distance Education in Brazil 2011. ABED – Associação Brasileira de Educação a Distância. Pearson Education do Brasil, São Paulo, 2012.
16. More can be seen at: http://neoprospecta.com/. Accessed January 2013.
17. Use of the logo authorized by the enterprise.
18. As can be seen at: http://www.bccresearch.com/. Accessed January 2013.
19. As can be seen at: http://www.marketresearch.com/Business-Insights-v893/Future-Molecular-Diagnostics-Innovative-technologies-2729698/. Accessed January 2013.
20. As can be seen at: http://www.sapienspark.com.br/. Accessed January 2013.
21. As seen at: http://www.bloomberg.com/billionaires/. Accessed February 2013.
22. As seen at: http://www.estudar.org.br/?idioma = 1. Accessed February 2013.
23. As seen at: http://www.endeavor.org.br/. Accessed February 2013.
24. As seen at: http://www.fundacaolemann.org.br/. Accessed February 2013.
25. As seen at: https://lemanncenter.stanford.edu/. Accessed February 2013.

# CHAPTER 8

## Case Studies in England

*Without tradition, art is a flock of sheep without a shepherd. Without innovation, it is a corpse.*

(Winston Churchill, 1874—1965)[1]

Josiah Wedgwood is considered by many to be the archetypal innovator (Dodgson and Gann, 2010). In addition to his pioneering work in bridging the scientific and artistic communities by developing a new approach to industrial design in relation to the manufacture of pottery, and being the founder of the Wedgwood Company, he was responsible for improvements to the quality of life and work in the society in which he lived. He was a prominent abolitionist and the grandfather of Charles Darwin. He was also, some have suggested, the most impressive and refined example of an innovator who synthesized research and technological expertise with a deep appreciation of market demand. In this chapter we provide examples from the second of our national cases, England, which illustrates how the country is attempting to rebuild long-term trust between the financial, productive and academic sectors through the development of innovatory products. These examples are: Teaching Shakespeare at Stratford-upon-Avon; The Extended Project at Rugby School; Team Engineering at the Open University; Work-based Learning at the Institute of Education, University of London; and *Think, Play and Do* at Imperial College, University of London.

## 8.1 TEACHING SHAKESPEARE AT STRATFORD-UPON-AVON

William Shakespeare[2] was born in Stratford-upon-Avon, England, baptized on 26 April 1564, and died on 23 April 1616 in the same town. He was a poet and playwright, recognized as the greatest writer in the English language, and one of the world's most important dramatists. Shakespeare wrote plays that capture the complete range of human emotion and conflict, and they have been translated into every major living language. The plays are performed more often than those of any other playwright.

The Royal Shakespeare Company[3] (also known as the RSC) is based at Stratford-upon-Avon, Warwickshire, and has, as its principal activity, performances of the works of Shakespeare, his contemporaries and new playwrights. In addition, the RSC promotes educational activities and develops creative links with theatre professionals and interested teachers all over the world. In November 2010, the RSC re-opened its new theatres following a 4-year transformation project, and this made it possible to focus on its educational mission. Both the new Royal Shakespeare Theatre and Swan Theatre include a thrust stage (also known as an open stage) configuration, bringing the actors and audience closer together.

One of the educational programmes that the RSC is directly involved in promoting is the *Teaching Shakespeare*[4] project, in partnership with the University of Warwick[5]. This programme includes specially-created online resources and digital technology courses that exemplify the RSC's playful and creative approach to teaching and learning. This innovative educational approach allows classroom work to imitate the best rehearsal rooms, where active and collaborative exploration of Shakespeare's plays encourage young people to make powerful discoveries about themselves and each other, and how they can understand and interpret the world they live in. This experience is followed by a tailor-made set of online practitioner resources, giving teachers unique access to a tried and tested rehearsal room approach to teaching Shakespeare.

The accredited courses and practitioner resources provide additional academic support for teachers. The programmes are designed for experienced teachers, as well as those beginning their professional careers, and theatre practitioners, working with students aged 8 and above. In particular, *Teaching Shakespeare* aims to appeal to English, Arts and Theatre teachers working with 11–16-year-olds, as well as teachers of 8–11-year-olds who specialize in literacy development. *Teaching Shakespeare* also provides an invaluable resource for teachers working with international students aged 16–18, who may be studying Shakespeare for the first time.

There are clear educational benefits resulting from the development programme for teachers, enabling them to teach Shakespeare more effectively. It also contributes to broadening and deepening their subject knowledge, allowing them to enjoy their teaching more and helping them to build better relationships with their students. There is some evidence to suggest that these programmes encourage the development of transferable skills, so that the skills and dispositions learnt on the *Teaching Shakespeare* programmes can be applied to other areas of the curriculum. These programmes have the added advantage of drawing attention to the timeliness of great art, and the sense in which some universal values can transcend place and time.

The RSC has produced a toolkit[6] that provides primary and secondary teachers with ideas on how to creatively introduce Shakespeare into the classroom and engage learners of all abilities. The lessons are inspired by the way the RSC works in the rehearsal room, which is conceived of as just another *kind of room*. Learning experiences can be as varied and rich as the texts themselves, and even transcend those texts by exploring the world while, at the same time, enhancing their key life skills. The toolkit for teachers is composed of ten units. Units 1–6 introduce active teaching and learning methods that are suitable for focusing on any of Shakespeare's plays, although *Romeo and Juliet* has been adopted as the principal teaching text. In particular, Unit 6 is dedicated to other plays like *Hamlet, Macbeth* and *A Midsummer Night's Dream*. Units 7–9 explore the contextual and theoretical aspects of active learning, and Unit 10 offers a broader perspective on learning, and emphasizes the continuing value of teaching Shakespeare across the world. For each unit, teachers are asked to complete entries in their personal learning journals.

By exploring the creative potential of their students, and managing student behaviour and relationships through the use of advanced teaching skills by questioning in an active and collaborative way, teachers are creating learning environments that allow students to make their own informed choices. These approaches are modelled on the principles underpinning independent and transformative pedagogies as outlined in Chapter 6. What is also interesting are the similarities and commonalities that can be observed between these teaching and learning classroom approaches, and the way the theatre company actually works in production. So, there are similarities between the two collaborative processes: the director and his or her actors rehearsing a play *and* a teacher and his or her students exploring a text together. In both cases, the director or the teacher works as an enabler with the intention of promoting discovery learning by using advanced questioning skills. The adopted *modus operandi* is ensemble, where members of a group learn from each other and learn by doing. In general, the pedagogical activities stimulate reflection on texts and performances.

The teachers involved do not have to be Shakespearean specialists. They are advised to start from where they are confortable and work from there. Previous experience has suggested that the best learning takes place when teachers are slightly out of their comfort zone; and, as long as they share those feelings in an appropriate way, their students will follow them. Active approaches improve student attitudes to Shakespeare and have a significant impact on their attainment. For example, in a controlled experiment, students who were taught in a rehearsal room setting showed significant improvements in their attitude towards Shakespeare as well as in their overall attitude to school. Additionally, there is some evidence of statistically significant increases in attainment in literacy, communication and interpersonal skills[4].

The online resource for *Teaching Shakespeare* is divided into ten units of study, where the core of each unit is a set of films, supported by podcasts and activities that guide the teacher through a key area of practice. The unit structure always contains an introductory page, helping the teacher to navigate through the material and a concluding page reflecting on the learning. The introductory page contains an overview of the learning objectives, a list of the chapters and related film content, links to all the activities and resources that are modelled and discussed, recorded podcasts, and a series of questions to guide reflections in the teacher's personal learning journal. The concluding page contains: a summary of the learning, suggestions for further reading and resources, additional podcasts, and recommended actions to consolidate the learning. These resources and the pedagogies that are encouraged, offer an approach which fits with independent and transformatory learning.

## 8.2 THE EXTENDED PROJECT AT RUGBY

Another interesting case where independent learning approaches have been used is the extended project piloted at Rugby School[7], which is an educational community institution whose philosophy embraces the challenges of academic excellence, responsibility and leadership, spiritual awareness and participation in a wide variety of activities. At Rugby the main target is to transform boys' and girls' individual talents into accomplishments, which allow them to be valued and respected in an increasingly complex world.

Rugby School has been in existence for more than two centuries, and is known as the place where rugby football was invented (see Figure 8.1). Nowadays, the School is also a tourist site for visitors as the "home of the game", and rugby teams from all over the world can be seen training in front of the distinctive backdrop of Butterfield's Chapel. Rugby School tries to combine tradition with state-of-the-art educational resources, so that every pupil has a laptop and every classroom is equipped with an interactive electronic whiteboard in a high-tech, wireless-networked, whole-School learning environment.

*Perspective on Science*[8] is a course delivered over 1 or 2 years. The course is offered as a Designed Programme within the Extended Project to enable students to research ethical and philosophical issues in relation to science. It is extremely popular both with science and humanities students. Within the course, students are encouraged to explore approaches to critical reading of sources, philosophical thinking skills, philosophical questions and ethical arguments, as well as the promotion of discussion and debate, management of student research

*Figure 8.1 The Rugby School, where the Rugby sport was invented.*

projects, and assessment within the Extended Project framework (Taylor, 2012). The course leader is Dr John Taylor, who is the *Perspective on Science* Director and Chief Examiner for Extended Projects.

The whole programme is designed around a philosophy of independent learning. The course structure comprises two topics: (i) analytical skills, taught through historical research, philosophical frameworks/thinking skills and ethical thinking; and (ii) the completion of a research project, focusing on research proposal planning, writing and editing, and finally presentation. The programme is taught by a cross-curricular team and thus has many of the characteristics of an integrated learning programme.

Fogarty (1994) has identified ten models of curriculum integration and these range from strongly classified and strongly framed curricula, as in the traditional approach, to weakly classified and weakly framed networked approaches to curriculum planning. Between the two extremes: *traditional or fragmented* and *networked approaches*, she identifies eight other points on the continuum: connected, nested, sequenced, shared, webbed, threaded, integrated and immersed. In her book *The Mindful School: How to Integrate the Curriculum*, Fogarty (*ibid.*) provides more detail about these different approaches.

A *fragmented curriculum* has clear boundaries between the different subjects, and thus this first type cannot reasonably be thought of as integrated. Subject delineations are clear-cut, they are taught in separate blocks on the timetable, they have their own formal knowledge structure, and content is treated as distinctive and belonging to the specific area. In a *connected curriculum*, reference is made to other content areas, connections are sought and suggestions are made as to how knowledge in another domain can supplement and contribute to knowledge in the specified domain. A *nested curriculum* has some similarities; however, a clear distinction is made between generic skills and specific content. This form is only partially integrated as the content of the subject area is still treated as specific to a curriculum area; however, some common skills are identified which cross the boundaries between different content areas and these are taught across the curriculum.

Further along the continuum, is a reference point that we might want to describe as *sequenced*. Here, deliberately planned topics are arranged to be taught at the same time, so that learners moving between different subject areas are taught the same concept—albeit that reference is made to a different application and a different discipline in two or more different contexts. For example, statistical probability is taught in Mathematics as well as in Social Science. This reinforces the learning of the concept, and allows students to understand how it can be used in different contexts. The next point on the continuum is where the curriculum can be thought of as *shared*. Here, a particular topic that has a number of different disciplinary strands, is chosen. Teachers from different subject disciplines are partnered and teach different aspects of the topic.

A *webbed curriculum* is very similar to a shared curriculum; the difference being that there is a greater degree of integration. The curriculum is divided into themes, and each theme is treated in a different way by different subject teachers. Thus the integrity of each discipline is retained, and the methods and approaches that are distinctive to these disciplines are taught—even if the generic subject matter is the same. Next to it on the continuum is a *threaded curriculum*, where the emphasis is on the process of learning, or on what might be called a meta-theoretical process. The content is subordinated to the teaching of these skills, and a curriculum that cuts across the traditional disciplines and focuses on common skills is devised. In this scenario, the traditional and highly classified curriculum is abandoned for a new set of delineations and boundaries, based around different types of skill. Clearly within each discipline the traditional curriculum skills were featured—however, these skills were content specific. A threaded curriculum offers a weakly classified curriculum in that skills and content are treated as separate. A threaded curriculum in turn gives way to an *integrated curriculum*. Here disciplinary boundaries begin to dissolve, as teachers work in inter-disciplinary teams to plan units round overlapping concepts and themes.

Almost at one end of the continuum is *immersion*. Here, integration becomes the responsibility of the learner as he or she focuses on a particular topic or theme, and borrows from different disciplines, ideas, theories, skills and the like. There is little evidence here of any adherence to the methods and protocols embedded within particular disciplines. The disciplines themselves are treated as impediments to the development of knowledge, and this strong classification is transgressively dissolved. This finally, gives way to a *networked curriculum*. Kysilka (1998: 199) suggests that such an approach "requires learners to reorganize relationships of ideas within and between the separate disciplines, as well as ideas and learning strategies within and between learners".

Each of these forms of integration can be positioned along a continuum (see Figure 8.2) with a fragmented curriculum being strongly classified and framed, in contrast to networking approaches to curriculum planning which are weakly classified and weakly framed. Taylor's model of cross-curricularity and integration fits better with networking approaches than with programmes of learning that are more strongly classified and framed.

A key pedagogical approach adopted is *dialogic confrontation.* As Levinson *et al.* (2008) suggests: "(d)iversity, passionate advocacy and positioning of extreme points of view are characteristics of good discussion. While passion and extreme points of view can sometimes appear intimidating to other students, teachers ought not to be unduly worried, indeed such characteristics can be harnessed for productive discussion". Students are expected to produce a research report and present the main findings to their peers. The research report has to contain: an abstract, an introduction, a literature review, a discussion, and a set of conclusions. A sample timeline is provided for the students, as well as a protocol for developing and assessing oral presentation skills. An abstract of up to 250 words is required to summarize the report with a focus on its purpose, findings and conclusions. The introduction, up to 750 words, should include: (i) an explanation of the project research question; (ii) the rationale for the choice of the question; (iii) an identification of the ethical and philosophical aspects of the research question; (iv) an outline of the relevant science involved; and (v) an explanation of key terms used in the project.

The literature review, up to 2200 words, should contain an outline of the scientific literature that underlies the project, stating key dates,

*Figure 8.2 Curricular modes in a continuum.*

developments and the people involved. There is also a requirement to contextualize these developments and discuss the influences on the key figures, including the reliability of the sources. The discussion, up to 3000 words, should provide a reasoned answer to the research question initially posed by the student, with his or her point of view clearly stated. The student is expected to consider all possible arguments both in favour and against what is being proposed. The student is also encouraged to provide a reflection on the research process that he or she has undertaken, and give some indication of the limitations of the study and how his or her ideas developed.

This is a form of enquiry-based learning, and another example is a new Master's module: "Teaching for Independent Student Inquiry (ISI)"[9], at the Institute of Education, University of London, planned for October 2013. ISI is a 30-credit Master's module which sits within the MTeach programme at the Institute of Education (IoE) and can be transferred to other Master's courses, particularly in education. It is a distance-learning course, providing regular opportunities for online collaborative inquiry with fellow students and tutors. It is aimed at practitioners of Extended Project Qualifications and Critical Thinking, with an emphasis on the philosophical underpinnings of student inquiry, critical thinking and writing, and on supporting independent inquiry.

Enquiry-Based Learning (EBL) is a teaching and learning approach in which learning is driven by a process of enquiry owned by the student. Starting with a "scenario" and with the guidance of a facilitator, students identify their own issues and questions. They then examine the resources they need to research the topic, thereby acquiring the requisite knowledge. This knowledge so gained is more readily retained because it has been acquired through experience and in relation to a real-life problem. The principles that underpin this mode of learning are:

- Learning is student-centred, with an emphasis on group work and the use of library, web and other information resources.
- Lecturers become facilitators, providing encouragement and support to enable the students to take responsibility for what and how they learn.
- Students reach a point where they are not simply investigating questions posed by others, but can formulate their own research topics and convert that research into useful knowledge.

- Students gain not only a deeper understanding of the subject matter, but also the knowledge-development and leadership skills required for tackling complex problems that occur in the real world.
- Fundamentally, students are more engaged with the subject. Learning is perceived as being more relevant to their needs, and as a result they are motivated and ready to learn.
- Students can expand on what they have learned by following their own research interests.
- Enquiry-based learning allows students to develop a more flexible approach to their studies, giving them the freedom and the responsibility to organize their own pattern of work within the time constraints of the task.
- Working within and communicating to a group are vital for a student's employability.
- Self-directed learning not only develops key skills for postgraduate study, but also leads to original thought that contributes to larger research projects, papers and publications.
- For teaching staff, developing an enquiry-based learning module helps them to understand the learning process and the changing needs of their students.

## 8.3 TEAM ENGINEERING AT THE OPEN UNIVERSITY

The Open University (OU)[10] is considered a world leader in modern distance learning. It is seen as one of the pioneers of teaching and learning methods that enable people to achieve their career and life goals—studying at times and in places to suit them. Its mission is to be open to people, places, methods and ideas, making learning resources available at a low cost without sacrificing quality. The idea of an OU was mooted in the first part of the twentieth century, when the educationist J.C. Stobart, in 1926, wrote a memo, while working for the British Broadcast Corporation (BBC)[11], advocating a wireless university. Nevertheless, it wasn't until the early 1960s that such an idea took concrete form, when the BBC and the Ministry of Education started to discuss proposals for a *College of Air* in relation to programmes of adult education. In 1963 Lord Taylor, chairman of a Labour Party study group, presented a report about the exclusion from higher education of people from lower income groups. The Labour Party won the election in 1964, and in 1966 Labour's general election manifesto contained a commitment to establish the *University of the Air*. In May

1969, Professor Walter Perry was appointed as the OU's first Vice-Chancellor, and the university was transferred to a small country estate in the new city (less than 2 years old) of Milton Keynes. Finally, in 1971 the OU was opened offering a new type of education.

During the 1970s the OU was finally accepted as a part of the university sector, and the 1980s were years of expansion and consolidation. In the 1990s, the OU delivered video teaching by DVD, and from the mid-1990s began to intensify its use of the internet, becoming a world leader in innovative teaching methodologies using digital technologies. Undergraduate and Graduate Engineering were seen as areas of intense interest, where technology could combine with human ingenuity to deliver new possibilities to educate professionals for innovation.

The Course, *Team Engineering* (known internally as T885)[12], is an interesting example of an independent learning initiative and aims to develop, amongst others, the essential professional engineering skill of working with others. The students work as part of a small project team, formed at the first compulsory weekend residential school. Projects encompass a broad sweep of engineering functions, requiring the co-operative development of knowledge and skills needed to analyse an engineering system and produce a revised specification for that system. They work together in a team via email, telephone and flash meeting, under guidance from their tutor. The team's results are presented and assessed at the second residential weekend school and through submission of a written report. The Course is the last requirement of study to obtain an Open University postgraduate qualification in Engineering. The intention is to draw together all the previous knowledge and skills learnt during previous periods of study, by introducing a new element into the student curriculum: working with other people to accomplish a common goal.

The principal driver behind *Team Engineering* is that most engineering work nowadays is completed in teams, and this contrasts with previous traditions of working alone. Thus, the main objectives of the course are to: (i) develop the capability of working with others, especially in teams, which is considered essential for professional engineers; (ii) create the opportunity to practise information retrieval and empirical research skills; (iii) develop the capacities to design engineering systems to meet client demands; and (iv) learn to collectively evaluate an engineering system in the economic, social and environmental context in which the task must be performed[13].

The students learn by working in teams to solve problems related to at least three elements: (i) the functional aspects of the problem for which they have to take individual responsibility within the team; (ii) the team role aspects related to the team functions for which they take responsibility; and (iii) by acknowledging their own strengths and weaknesses and recognizing those of their team members, learning to divide the tasks in such a way as to obtain the desired results. The development of these skills, it is surmised, benefits the professional engineer in his or her future professional activities. The Course is based on the idea that in an academic project, the process is more important than the final product; it is the journey, not the destination, of learning that is more important.

In the programme, there are two residential weekends. During the first of the residential weekends, the first activities comprise: (i) learning about the theories underpinning working with others; (ii) reviewing their learning preferences; (iii) spending time getting to know other students on the same course; (iv) reviewing the available project options; (v) forming a team around a particular project; and (vi) developing a project plan for the team. During this residential weekend, students are required to develop understandings about: (i) individual team members and other people's styles in discussion; (ii) the ways in which a consensus can be reached in the team; and (iii) the different roles adopted by different members of the team. Following the first residential weekend, the students use the next twenty weeks to keep in close touch with other team members to review and update their project plans, if they think that this is necessary, staying in regular and frequent contact with each other and with the tutor.

At the end of this period, the members of the team meet together for a second residential weekend, when they are required to: (i) draw together their work into a draft final team report; (ii) make team presentations of their findings; (iii) review the performances of members of their team and the individual contributions to them; and (iv) develop a plan for completing and submitting their team reports and individual reports for formative assessments. They now have ten weeks to complete the writing up of their projects, and they are then required to submit it for formal and summative assessment.

The learning outcome expected from those completing the Course is associated with the following knowledge, understanding and competence elements: (i) familiarity with the essential concepts, and an understanding of their relationship to the engineering world in the context of decisions they take whilst completing their projects; (ii) an understanding of the scientific and mathematical principles related to the chosen project; (iii) a knowledge of business practices and of design processes and methodologies used in finding solutions to the problems they have been presented with; (iv) a knowledge of the historical aspects and new technologies connected with their projects; and (v) clear competence in associated cognitive, practical and professional skills.

In summary, the Course *Team Engineering* comprises a fresh examination of social, environmental, ethical, economic and commercial aspects, provides an academic curriculum that prepares professionals for understanding clients' needs and creates innovative solutions to those needs. Making intense use of digital technologies, the students are stimulated to communicate effectively through written and spoken language, developing their capabilities to collectively work as a team. Above all, the most important characteristic to be developed is how to continue to learn independently and especially not to fear novel situations.

## 8.4 WORD-BASED LEARNING AT THE INSTITUTE OF EDUCATION

The IoE is the only college of the University of London dedicated entirely to education and the United Kingdom's leading centre for studies in education, training teachers and related disciplines. Its reputation has been gained and sustained over a period of more than 100 years. The staff includes world scholars and active researchers. Together with a large range of students, it contributes to an intellectually rich learning community, which reflects cultural diversity as well as varied political, philosophical and methodological positions on educational and social scientific thinking[14].

Founded in October 1902 as the London Day Training College (LDTC), under the joint auspices of the University of London and the London County Council, in 1932, it became the University's largest central activity as the Institute of Education. From 1949 it acquired a dual role at the centre of a wider Institute of some 30 associated colleges and departments of education. During this period it was responsible for the education and training of one in four new teachers in England and Wales. Following the demise of the Area Training Organizations (ATOs) in the 1970s, the Institute reverted to its previous role. In 1987 the award of a royal charter set the seal upon its status as an independent college and school of the University of London. The IoE became a member of the 1994 Group[15] of 19 leading research intensive United Kingdom universities. The Group was established in 1994 to promote excellence in university research and teaching. The IoE's academic structure is faculty-based, with two Faculties, the Faculty of Children and Learning and the Faculty of Policy and Society, and, in addition, the Doctoral School. The reach of international engagement extends to some 100 countries through collaborative partnerships with governments, international and national agencies, institutions and organizations in every continent.

Work-based learning is understood as a process where the problem to be solved originates from and within the work environment—this makes the assumption that the problem is the starting point of learning. This requires the development of a well-designed problem-learning approach (Hmelo-Silver, 2004; Sockalingam *et al.*, 2011). The following additional characteristics are also important: (i) learning is strongly dependent on student ownership of the problem and solution; (ii) it demands a particular type of support from the tutor, because their roles are considerably different from teachers in a conventional learning environment; (iii) the number of lectures is limited; (iv) in general, small-group collaboration is needed; and (v) ample time for self-study is made available.

Many students have trouble making the transition to the more independent learning style required at university compared with their previous place of study. University study requires students to take responsibility for their own learning, to be more self-directed, to make decisions about what they will focus on and how much time they will spend on learning both inside and outside the classroom. This transition may be especially difficult for international students who may be used to more support and direction, and even "parent-like" relationships with their teachers at university. It will be useful for them (and all students) to know precisely how they are responsible for their learning in the new setting. This will require them to understand that they need to play a more active role in their own learning, and will require greater self-motivation, organization, and greater self-awareness (metacognition) of their learning needs and behaviour.

The Work-based Learning for Educational Professionals Centre (WLE) is a Higher Education Funding Council for England (HEFCE) initiative to encourage excellence and innovation in Higher Education. The Centre was part of the National Centre for Excellence in Teaching and Learning Languages (CETL) initiative between 2005 and 2010. The WLE aims to develop new approaches to work-based learning through facilitating innovations in: learning at work and through professional practice; teaching and assessment modes for work-related and work-located learning; and the uses of e-learning and digital technologies. In addition, the Centre has focused on interdisciplinary approaches and international collaborations, contributing to the development of new conceptual and theoretical approaches to work-based learning.

The Centre offers an interesting example of an independent learning approach and the use of new technologies for teaching and learning, it has also contributed to the development of understanding of work-based learning and informal practice. The educational framework associated with the activities in the CETL programme was based on a theory of change, which is understood as "a systematic and cumulative study of the links between activities, outcomes and context of the initiative" (Connel and Kubish, 1998). The adopted principles of reward and recognition were: excellent teaching produces excellent learning; recognizing individual and institutional excellence in teaching and learning; promoting excellence across the sector; and providing a relatively light steer on specific designs for excellence. The WLE was responsible for more than one hundred projects over 5 years, and the key resources built over the 5-year programme included: intellectual and academic capital through a dynamic of research projects informing pedagogical practices and contributing to theory-building in work-based learning; physical and virtual centres supporting activities in face-to-face, mixed-mode and at a distance; and a multi-faceted approach to dissemination with a multifunctional website centre[16] stimulating the development of communities of practice.

The main strands of the Centre's activities were identified by Carpentier (2011). These focused on the role played by work-based learning in different areas, the connections with independent forms of learning and the appropriate uses of digital technologies. Among the case studies adopted by Carpentier (2011), two of them are described below. The first of these was the project "Putting Knowledge to Work" (PKTW), and it focused on the idea of how learning can be transferred from theory into practice. The knowledge generated and practiced in one context needs to be recontextualized in order for it to be used in new and different contexts. Evans *et al.* (2010, 2011) explore the nature of this recontextualization process with particular reference to how concepts and practices change as they are used in different contexts.

Another interesting WLE project was "Mobile Learning", which was implemented by the London Mobile Learning Group (LMLG) as a way of developing new work-based approaches in learning through innovative uses of digital technologies. This project demanded an inter-disciplinary approach involving areas such as sociology, pedagogy, educational technology, design and cultural and media studies. It is remarkable to observe that the project started in 2007, and at that time mobile learning was just emerging as a real possibility in terms of educational use. The LMLG developed a general theoretical and conceptual framework, taking into account the use of mobile technologies in social, cultural and economic contexts, as well as the way they are embedded in everyday lives. The group collected evidence about how e-learning and digital media impacted on student experiences (Pachler and Daly, 2011). The group also explored the use of mobile devices to provide just-in-time remote mentor support in the context of workplace learning in the hospital sector. Learners were strongly encouraged to explore independent learning and the use of new technologies to the upper limit of their capabilities.

Mobile devices were improved by web-enabled smart phones, which provide users with full access to information wherever and whenever they need it. Students are able to collect data and have access to institutional learning environments, besides watching a class or following an experiment in a laboratory. Additionally, more recent mobile phones are context-aware, with GPS positioning, recognition of objects by infrared or wireless tags, and automatic interpretation of images.

There is a great deal of further research work needed with regards to mobile learning, especially in relation to the work environment, and the Centre's work contributed to understanding how education and technology can be connected productively in particular environments. These two cases and other initiatives sponsored by the WLE represent important opportunities to develop deeper understandings of work-based learning, where independent learning approaches, as educational methodologies, and technology-enhanced teaching, as educational tools, were used at all phases of the project, and they constitute interesting examples of how to meet the diversity of professional learning needs.

## 8.5 *THINK, PLAY AND DO* AT IMPERIAL COLLEGE

Imperial College London[17], confirmed as being consistently rated amongst the world's best universities, is a science-based institution with a reputation for excellence in teaching and research. Among the units forming the institution, there is the Imperial College Business School hosting many research programmes and offering MBA, MSc, and undergraduate programmes, as well as executive courses. Among the research groups, the Innovation and Entrepreneurship Group[18] has a reputation for international excellence, characterized by a unique insight into the latest practices to make innovation happen by working closely with businesses, government and other academic institutions. The Group, through a special capability to explore inter-disciplinary applications, leads research into processes involving the launching of new ideas requiring an array of entrepreneurial, research, design and commercialization skills, as well as the ability to extract value from these ideas. The Group was founded by David Gann[19], who also co-founded the *Think, Play and Do* Group, an Imperial College London spin-off specializing in innovation strategy and management.

Dodgson *et al.* (2005) use the expression *innovation technology* (IvT) to describe a new technology category, resulting from state-of-the-art digital technologies, which include simulation and modelling tools, virtual reality, data mining, and rapid prototyping. They distinguish IvT from traditional information and communication technology, also from operation and manufacturing technology, and argue that the changes associated with the adoption of IvT leads to the intensification of innovation. They also assume that IvT is associated with an innovation process that can be better characterized as *thinking, playing, and doing*.

Thinking is affected by IvT via new tools like those supporting e-science, allowing the formation of virtual research communities and making it easier to find and combine information through data searching, including recent developments in data mining and artificial intelligence. Data mining is enabled by the easy-to-use, intuitive navigation and search tools permitting huge amounts of information to be collected in several databases, and contributing to making sense and deriving patterns from raw material that previously, without these tools, was unobservable or incomprehensible. To help manage the data and to support the decision-making steps in the innovation processes, artificial intelligence protocols have been increasingly adopted.

Playing is transformed by simulation, modelling, and visualization technologies, making use of IvT platforms, such as computer-aided design (CAD) and the developing capacities of virtual reality. The time-wasting approaches of drafting, physical testing, and model building applied to many traditional design tasks have been replaced by simulation and modelling. As a result, it has been possible to provide simplified representations of a system, which are used in a wide range of engineering tasks, including tests, analysis, diagnostics and design optimization. Virtual reality tools are helping designers to bridge the gap between scientists and other professionals, integrating the processes of thinking, playing and doing in the innovation process. Modelling and simulation tools have been used extensively by scientists and enterprises in a wide range of ways, from climate modelling to financial simulations, but their use has been restricted in education until recently.

Change is accelerating due to the recent development of rapid prototyping technologies constructed upon existing design and manufacturing systems. Rapid prototyping is the production of physical three-dimensional (3D) solid objects from CAD design, enabling the examination of a variety of design concepts before the final design is fixed. Rapid prototyping kits in the form of 3D printers are likely to become available at home and in schools, allowing new possibilities and changing our day-by-day activities and influencing the way we teach and learn. With modelling and simulation, associated with other state-of-the-art digital technological tools, the trend is towards personal customization. Advances in CAD design and 3D printing will allow firms to make products that are individually tailored to each customer—in order to produce precisely the tool they need or want. For little more than the price of a mass-produced object, everyone will get exactly what they need.

Most of the problems to be solved in the future will demand thinking across different traditional academic disciplines, with the majority of them at the interface of different fields of research. As Dodgson *et al.* (2005) have pointed out, IvT has the capacity to assist communication and understanding across disciplines. This may prove to be one of the new technology's principal benefits, contributing to breaking down artificial barriers and to a new technology fusion, a necessary step in the innovation processes. *Think, play, and do* is much more compatible with a model of a circle connecting science, technology and innovation, as we have suggested in this book, rather than sequential and linear traditional models.

To promote innovative ideas and to create new opportunities, enterprises will need to respond to the development of new technologies. Entrepreneurs will increasingly need to focus more on integrating technologies, and the development of products and processes that require a more disciplined approach. Citizens in general will be required to develop better understanding of the new technological processes and be prepared to use and feel comfortable with new technologies. The educational process that this implies will not be easy to effect.

## NOTES

1. As seen at: http://www.brainyquote.com/quotes/keywords/innovation.html#mOrDtb6A1RSFsasx.99. Accessed March 2013.
2. As seen at: http://absoluteshakespeare.com/trivia/biography/shakespeare_biography.htm. Accessed March 2013.
3. As seen at: http://www.rsc.org.uk/. Accessed March 2013.
4. As seen at: http://www.teachingshakespeare.ac.uk/. Accessed March 2013.
5. As seen at: http://www2.warwick.ac.uk/. Accessed March 2013.
6. The RSC Shakespeare Toolkit for Teachers, An Active Approach to Bringing Shakespeare's plays alive in the Classroom. Published by Methuen Drama, 2010.
7. As seen at: http://www.rugbyschool.net/. Accessed February 2013.
8. As seen at: http://www.rugbyschool.net/The-Perspectives-Model-for-the-Extended-Projects-Dissertation. Accessed February 2013.

9. As seen at: http://www.edexcel.com/quals/project/organisations/Pages/ioe.aspx. Accessed February 2013.
10. As seen at: http://www.open.ac.uk/. Accessed March 2013.
11. As seen at: http://www.bbc.co.uk/. Accessed March 2013.
12. As seen at: http://www3.open.ac.uk/study/postgraduate/course/t885.htm. Accessed March 2013.
13. T885 Team Engineering Module Guide. The Open University, 2010.
14. As seen at: http://www.ioe.ac.uk/index.html. Accessed March 2013.
15. As seen at: http://www.1994group.ac.uk/. Accessed March 2013.
16. As seen at: www.wlecentre.ac.uk. Accessed March 2013.
17. As seen at: http://www3.imperial.ac.uk/. Accessed March 2013.
18. As seen at: http://www3.imperial.ac.uk/business-school. Accessed March 2013.
19. As seen at: http://www3.imperial.ac.uk/people/d.gann. Accessed March 2013.

# CHAPTER 9

# Conclusions

*We want to have certainties and no doubt—results and no experiences—without even seeing that the certainties can arise only through doubts and results only through experiences.*

(Carl G. Jung, 1875–1961)[1]

In this book we have been concerned with the changing roles of universities (and marginally schools) in relation to the development of creative, inclusive, participatory and independent pedagogies for the delivery of an innovation agenda. Peter Scott (2000) identifies five features of the late-modern world: acceleration and turn-over, simultaneity and time–space compression, increasing risk, non-linearity, and reflexivity. To these we can add five more: normalization and individualization, the marginalization of traditional forms of knowledge and the relocation of power bases, control being exercised at a distance by governing elites, compartmentalization, and the commodification of knowledge. The university itself is increasingly being influenced by policy-driven interventions by the state, new forms of communication including digital technologies and multimodal forms of expression, its marginalization from the centre of the knowledge industry, "non-jurisdictionally bounded global discourses" (Yeatman, 1990), and by crises in disciplinarity and professionalism.

The first of Scott's features, acceleration and turn-over, refers to the increasing volume of technical, aesthetic and intellectual goods that are produced and made available in society, and the way these have a shorter and shorter lifespan. The second feature he refers to is the radical compression of time and space. In part, this has been brought about by the introduction of new technologies and globalizing processes. In part also, this has occurred because of the demands of the market and the subsequent mindset that is needed to compete successfully. Fuelled by the Internet and other technological compressors, this has had profound effects on human identities and relations. The third feature, for Scott, is increasing risk. At all levels of society, taking risks is now acceptable, with catastrophic consequences if the enterprise fails. Note the way a relatively small number of bankers have plunged North America and much of Europe into a profound economic crisis. The fourth feature identified by Scott is what he calls non-linearity, complexity and chaos, and this refers to the crisis in the legitimacy of knowledge and the way that knowledge is now endlessly revised and re-presented. Finally, he identifies, as a feature of the late-modern world that we now live in, the idea of reflexivity. What he means by this is that boundaries between producers and users of knowledge are weakened, knowledge foundations are discredited and shown to be expressions of particular valued interests, and it now becomes more difficult to identify whether we are making progress in society. The enlightenment dream that we referred to earlier is now thoroughly compromised.

As we suggested, to these we can add five more. The first is the way power strategies are becoming better understood and better able to be used. Disciplinary knowledge embedded in universities, for example, provides solace for its members and has powerful effects. In effect, the discipline works through processes of normalization and individualization. As Marshall (1990: 22) suggests: "the two most obvious meanings that can be given to the word 'discipline' seemingly separate are in fact closely entwined; a body of knowledge is a system of social control to the extent that discipline (knowledge) makes discipline (social control) possible and vice versa". The second is the relocation of power from traditional sources of authority to new ones. This is more than just the weakening of boundaries between forms of knowledge and between different types of knowledge producers and users; it is also about a marginalization of traditional sources of knowledge and influence (such as universities and democratically elected politicians), and a re-allocation of this power and influence to other bodies (such as multi-national corporations and unelected power elites) that have a different conception of what knowledge is and what its purposes are.

The third additional feature of late-modern societies is that control is now exercised at a distance by governing elites. This distancing from the actual locus of power is significant in so far as responsibility for failure of government policy can now be more easily directed towards those institutions that deliver the product (such as a school or a university) and diverted away from those who actually control the system (e.g., politicians). This distancing mechanism works by giving individual institutions the responsibility to order their own affairs, but then at the same time putting in place quasi-governmental institutions to monitor and evaluate their practices.

The fourth additional feature is compartmentalization. Here the person compartmentalizes aspects of his or her life. For example, an academic may profess to believe in radical and transformative views about how society works, but then, as a senior manager in the institution in which he or she works, adopt ways of working and arrangements for subordinates that both reinforce the status quo and contradict his or her own beliefs. Finally, there is the process of commodification in relation to knowledge. Here knowledge of processes, institutions and selves is reconfigured so that it can be sold in the market place. This constitutes, in effect, a significant epistemic reconstruction of the original knowledge that was produced. If we add together Scott's (*ibid.*) five features to our five additional ones, we should now have a better understanding of the way late-modern societies, such as the two case studies in this book (Brazil and England), function. Educational institutions, and in particular the academy, now have to cope with processes connected to rapid acceleration and turn-over, time−space compression, increasing risk, non-linearity, reflexivity, normalization and individualization, the marginalization of traditional forms of knowledge and the relocation of power bases, evaluation at a distance by governing elites, compartmentalization and commodification.

## 9.1 CREATIVITY AND INNOVATION

These ten features of late-modern societies are offered as the backdrop to the writing of this book. However, our principal concern all along has been to develop a creative, inclusive, participatory and independent pedagogy for the delivery of an innovation agenda. At the heart of any successful society is the learning capacity of its people both in the present and the future. The United Nations Development Programme argues that capacity relates not just to economic well-being but to other aspects of life.

> *Human Development is about much more than the rise and fall of national incomes. It is about creating an environment in which people can develop their full potential and lead productive, creative lives in accord with their needs and interests. People are the real wealth of nations. Development is thus about expanding the choices people have to lead lives they value. And it*

> is thus about much more than economic growth, which is only a means—if a very important one—of enlarging people's choices [...]. Fundamental to enlarging these choices is building human capabilities—the range of things that people can do or be in life. The most basic capabilities for human development are to lead long and healthy lives, to be knowledgeable, to have access to the resources needed for a decent standard of living and to be able to participate in the life of the community. Without these, many choices are simply not available, and many opportunities in life remain inaccessible.
> *(UNDP, 2009).*

Central then to capacity development is learning, at civic, institutional and individual levels, and in particular, its capacities, its affordances and its effects. In addition, there is a set of curriculum objectives or standards relating to the end-point or purpose of the educational process (at school, college or university level). These constitute an innovation agenda, which, we suggested, has the following features:

- It is a deliberate, temporary relaxation of rules, norms and arrangements of resources in order to explore the possibilities of alternative rules, norms and arrangements of resources.
- It is experimental and thus potentially has a high rate of failure.
- It comprises the re-visualization, re-modelling, re-representation and imaginative re-formation of everyday objects and practices.
- It encourages and legitimizes exploration across epistemic, ethical, disciplinary and practice boundaries.
- It has the potentiality to expand understandings of the self and others, and allow self-representations of past, future and counterfactual possibilities.
- It allows the development of fictional worlds and understandings of how these might impact on life worlds and the lifecourse.
- It is a trans-disciplinary, problem-solving, heterarchical and transient knowledge-producing activity.
- It has the potentiality to expand understandings of the possible functions and uses of an object.
- It is the successful application of ideas.

In this book we have examined the notion of innovation. Innovation, we suggested, is a key concept in the formation of modern societies. In the middle ages innovation meant novelty arising from human creativity, whereas today it has become emblematic of modern society and directly associated with the possibility of sustainable economic and social development. The concept of innovation is broader than simply technological innovation. More recently, a new wave of innovation approaches such as *open innovation, democratizing innovation, creative economies* and *organizational and marketing innovation* have been used in everyday and scientific discourse. Many of these are associated with new sites of production such as workplaces and homes, rather than traditional research laboratories and universities.

We also discussed the importance of innovation in contemporary society and the available new technologies that can be used in education. Our contention is that we are entering a third educational revolution, which implies that substantial changes are needed to the traditional ways that we teach and learn, as well as to how knowledge is produced and disseminated. We are now in a world where it is becoming clearer than ever that, despite the essential roles the traditional education systems have played, standard solutions and approaches are not appropriate for meeting new educational and social needs.

Capacity development then for a creative and innovatory agenda requires the development of a tailor-made pedagogy, which fits the contexts in which learning takes place. These contexts are geographical, cultural, epistemic and fundamentally relate to how that society arranges its resources and allocates its population to roles and positions of responsibility. In this book, we have focused on two such learning environments, Brazil and England. Both have different features and therefore require different types of pedagogy to accomplish the same end. However, what we can do is suggest, or at least sketch out, a framework for a common independent and transformative approach to teaching and learning.

There are a number of different terms that are used to describe independent learning, with perhaps the most common being "self-regulated learning". All these different terms have common features: learners have a meta-cognitive understanding of how they are learning; they are motivated to take responsibility for their learning; and they monitor and structure their own learning experiences. As is the case with many terms commonly used in higher education learning, "independent learning" can mean different things to different people, in different disciplines and in different cultures. This clearly places responsibility for learning on the student, aided by the teaching staff and defined by the limits and objectives of the programme, and more importantly, by the limitations built into the teaching and learning approaches, including the use of digital technologies.

## 9.2 NEW TECHNOLOGIES AND NEW PEDAGOGIES

In response then to these new technologies, there is an implicit demand for new teaching and learning approaches, which we might want to call independent and transformative learning pedagogies. However, there is a need in the first instance to understand what learning is and to develop a theory of learning, in order to develop a strategy for the capacity development of a population. Learning episodes have a set of features. The first of these, we suggested, is a determination of the circumstances in which learning can take place in the specific environment, and this includes all those cultural and epistemic differences between nations, systems of education and educational institutions. The second feature is a set of resources and technologies to allow that learning to take place, and this has both quantitative and qualitative dimensions (both how much resource there is and whether it is appropriate given the intended learning outcomes of the programme). The third feature is a particular type of relationship between teacher and learner to effect that learning; and this also requires a theory of learning, that is, an account of how the learning (expressed as a knowledge set, skill or disposition/inclination) can be actuated. The final feature of a learning environment is a theory of transfer, so that the learning or capacity development that takes place in a particular set of circumstances (for example, in an institution of higher education), with a set of learners, in a particular way, with a particular theory of learning underpinning it, and so forth, can transfer to environments in other places and times (cf. Scott *et al.*, 2012).

We also suggested that learning and capacity development can be theorized as a process, with a range of characteristics. It has a set of pedagogic relations; that is, it incorporates a relationship between a learner and a catalyst, which could be a person, an object in nature, an artefact, a particular array of resources, an allocation of a role or function to a person, a text, or a sensory object. A change process is required, either internal to the learner or external to the community of which this learner is a member. Each learning episode has socio-historical roots. What is learnt in the first place is formed in society and outside the individual. It is shaped by the life that the person is leading. It is thus both externally and internally mediated, and the form taken is determined by whether the process is cognitive, affective, meta-cognitive, conative or expressive. Finally, learning has an internalization element, where what is formally external to the learner is interiorized by the learner, and a performative element, where what is formally internal to the learner is exteriorized by the learner in the world (*ibid*).

This employs a Vygotskian framework and focuses on the notion of scaffolding (Vygotsky, 1978), which can operate, in different ways, in virtual and actual learning environments. Scaffolding in teaching essentially means an aid which is offered to the learner by a more experienced person (e.g., a teacher, mentor or pedagogic expert) in support of the learning process. This is not an easy concept to both understand and use in developing a learning environment. However, it has a number of features: it is supportive and temporary; it is offered to the learner in relation to specific tasks that he or she is asked to perform; the scaffold is dismantled at an appropriate time and in relation to the learning trajectory of the student; and the learner is unlikely to complete the task without it.

Despite its apparent simplicity, the broader notion of scaffolding in teaching is rather complex and its use in everyday teaching comes with a number of qualifications. The first of these is that there is no real agreement about what it means, and with regard to closely related mechanisms such as "contingency", "fading", and "transfer of responsibility" (cf., Van de Pol *et al.*, 2010). The second is that scaffolding is understood as a dynamic intervention, which is then adjusted (for better functioning) to accommodate the learner's ongoing progress. For these reasons, the amount and type of support given by the teacher depends on both the learning setting and how the student responds to the task. So, scaffolding operates differently in different situations and is not a one-size-fits-all technique. As a result, learning theorists are beginning to draw a distinction between the scaffold's means and its intentions. In real learning environments the extent and type of scaffolding is developed by the teacher, with some contribution by the learner. In virtual learning environments, in theory at least, the balance of responsibility for the construction and deployment of the scaffold has shifted towards the learner.

The Assessment for Learning movement (Black *et al.*, 2003) has captured some of these concerns, although at the moment it is more suited to actual rather than virtual learning environments. In addition, we suggested that it is flawed in three ways: the focus on formative assessment has inevitably marginalized processes of learning; as a result some of their strategies are both misapplied and misunderstood (for example, peer learning does not amount to asking students to make quantitative judgements about their colleague's work in relation to a set of criteria); and the reductive process for the purposes of quantifying and comparing results may have led to a distortion of the process of learning. Assessment for learning can be presented as five key strategies and one cohering idea. The five key strategies are: engineering effective classroom discussions, questions, and learning tasks; clarifying and sharing learning intentions and criteria for success; providing feedback that moves learners forward; activating students as the owners of their own learning; and activating students as instructional resources for one another. And the cohering idea is that evidence about student learning is used to adapt instruction to better meet learning needs; in other words, that teaching is adaptive to the student's learning needs (cf., Black *et al.*, 2003).

Learning environments are constructed in particular ways, with choices made at institutional and classroom levels about: pedagogic arrangements, relations between knowledge domains, knowledge or skill orientations, the knowledge frame, progression and pacing, relations between teacher and learner, relations between types of learners, spatial arrangements, temporal arrangements, and the criteria and means of evaluation. Above all else, the learning environment can be characterized by the type of learning that underpins the educational programme. What this means is that there are a series of elements that distinguish one type of learning environment from another; for example, a real learning environment can be distinguished from a virtual learning environment in a number of clear ways.

Virtual learning environments have a set of distinguishing features. Portability refers to the capacity of learners to choose where they study so they are not restricted, as they are in traditional forms of face-to-face learning, by having to be in one place, and incidentally at a particular time. Access to the learning environment is gained through a computer terminal, which can be carried around from place to place. Learning in a virtual learning environment allows a measure of flexibility, denied to those studying in traditional environments. This flexibility means that students have some control over when they study, where they study, for how long they study, at what times in their lives they study, and what they study. Although traditional learning environments try to build in flexible routes and pathways through the programme of learning, they are clumsy artefacts compared with a well-constructed virtual learning environment.

Transferability is another feature of virtual learning environments. This allows the student, as well as the teacher, to develop their skills beyond the physical environment of the classroom, widening access to education, and more importantly having the capacity to extend the range of pedagogic resources that are available in the learning setting, albeit that many of these resources are virtual. Another feature of a virtual learning environment is its capacity for interchangeability and subsequently, its ability to respond to changing circumstances and individual needs. So personalized programmes of learning can be more easily sustained in a virtual learning environment, than in a traditional face-to-face setting, and units and elements of the programme can be moved around to suit particular needs, thus creating new relations and connections between them.

Virtual learning environments allow a measure of student autonomy that even the best of traditional learning programmes have difficulty in offering. This is because virtual learning environments have the capacity to reconfigure the relationship between learner and stimulus. Instead of a form of textual production that privileges the writer over the reader, or in the case that we are considering here, the teacher over the learner, what we now have is the possibility, although it is rarely exploited, of this relationship becoming a much more equal one; that is, the reader and the writer, or the teacher and the learner, are now co-producers of texts, including learning texts or products. This new hypertextual model of representation has profound implications for the types of learning that can now be used and has been occasioned by the invention of digital technologies. It was Landow (1992: 70–1) who originally used the term: "this HyperTextual dissolution of centrality", and what he meant by this was that the new media allow the possibility of conversation rather than instruction, so that no one ideology or agenda dominated: "...the figure of the HyperText author approaches, even if it does not entirely merge with, that of the reader; the functions of reader and writer become more deeply inter-twined with each other than ever before".

## 9.3 EDUCATIONAL REFORM PROCESSES

We close this book by focusing on how best to implement educational reforms. Normally when a government decides to reform its educational system (or any other public service), it begins by surveying what is out there, on offer, and selecting what fits best in relation to that government's political leanings and the various constraints within which politicians operate. Although it is important to distinguish these approaches in order to clarify their potential to reach particular educational goals, their incarnation in real life settings is what determines their outcomes in the final instance. Thus, social participation in the United Kingdom during the 1980s had different meanings and outcomes to those experienced in Brazil in the same period. Sometimes, policies may grow organically out of previous ones or cohere easily with others in other sectors. However, in other cases they may be superimposed on, or make a sharp break from, what previously existed and may be assembled in an incoherent fashion, clashing with other educational or economic policies.

Currently on offer are four basic types or approaches to educational reform: top-down; market-driven; professional development; and social participation. The first of these is the top-down model. Governments stipulate how judgements should be made about the successful delivery of educational policies, and about how this should be achieved. They have the resources to impose these reforms on the system, although this is rarely achieved in practice in the way that policy-makers intend. The reason for this is that reform processes are generally multi-directional rather than uni-directional. Policy texts and directives are never complete, but always allow themselves to be over-written at every stage of the process and at every level (including the stages of implementation). This more fluid model of policy reform better reflects the relationship between policy development and implementation. A variant on this is an evaluative state model where the state withdraws from the precise implementation of policy reform, although it clearly has an important role in framing that policy. It sets up a series of semi-independent bodies whose purpose is to ensure that institutions, systems and individuals conform to government directives. These semi-independent bodies have a role in interpreting government policy and subsequently enforcing these policies by imposing sanctions on those educational institutions if they do not conform. The reform process is carried out by quasi-government agencies at arms-length from governments. This is, however, still very much a top-down reform model.

The second type is the quasi-market model. Here, governments decide to withdraw directly from the formation and implementation of policy, and set up quasi-market systems that hand power to the consumer, thus putting pressure on educational institutions by either exercising or threatening to exercise powers of voice or exit. If, in the latter case, too much of this takes place, then this threatens the survival of the organization. In this quasi-market model of reform, a currency is needed to allow consumers to make judgements between institutions to exercise voice or exit. In school systems around the world, a number of technologies have been proposed and tried out: the publication of examination and test results; the publication of value-added results taking account of prior achievement; and the publication of value-added results taking account of the different socio-economic circumstances of children. Each of these is likely to result in a different order of merit. Whichever approach is adopted, this works by making institutions responsive to a quasi-consumer interest, usually in the form of parental pressure. The market is a quasi-market, not least because some groups of consumers have a greater capacity to exercise voice or exit, and therefore have a greater degree of cultural capital and can display and use it more effectively than other people.

The third reform model is the professional development model. Here it is thought that different types of decisions within a system should be made by different people, because at the level at which they operate they are more likely to have the required expertise for making such decisions. The model rests on a notion of expertise so that better decisions are made by those whose knowledge of particular matters is superior to others. This expertise can be understood as a capacity to make correct decisions within specific contexts, having acquired those knowledge, skills and dispositions that are appropriate to the solving of problems within these contexts. This reform process, therefore, is driven by professional interests. It has come under sustained criticism for allowing vested interests to dominate and these values are considered to have superseded other more relevant values.

The final model is the social participation model, and the principle underpinning this is that because there are no absolute ways of determining the correctness of particular sets of values, decisions within education systems have to be made through negotiation between all the stakeholders. This means that no single stakeholder has a monopoly of power over any other, or can claim a special status, but the various partners negotiate with each other and come up with agreed solutions. What this also means is that the method for reaching agreement has to be, in some ideal sense, divested of those power relations that privilege one stakeholder over another. Governments in turn forsake their privileged position in the reform process, avoid sectionalism and properly enter into a deliberative process.

## NOTE

1. As cited by Joseph Campbell (1971).

# REFERENCES

Andrade, C.D., 1990. O Avesso das Coisas, Aforismos. Record, São Paulo.

Aubrey, B., Cohen, P., 1995. Working Wisdom: Timeless Skills and Vanguard Strategies for Learning Organizations. Jossey Bass, San Francisco.

Bandura, A., 1977. Social Learning Theory. General Learning Press, New York.

Barnett, R., 2007. A Will to Learn. Being a Student in an Age of Uncertainty. Open University Press, Berkshire.

Bell, F., 2011. Connectivism: its place in theory-informed research and innovation in technology-enabled learning. Int. Rev. Res. Open Dist. Learn. 12 (3), 98–118.

Bertazzo, J., 2012. A internacionalização do ensino superior como receita para o sucesso – a experiência do Reino Unido e sua relevância para o Brasil. Revista Mundo Afora (online).

Black, P., William, D., 1998. Inside the black box: raising standards through classroom assessment. Phi. Delta Kappan 80 (2), 139–148.

Black, P., Harrison, C., Lee, C., Marshall, B., William, D., 2003. Assessment for Learning: Putting it into Practice. Open University Press, Buckingham, UK.

Bredo, E., 1999. Reconstructing educational psychology. In: Murphy, P. (Ed.), Learners, Learning and Assessment. Sage Publications, London, pp. 23–45.

Bruner, J., 1996. The Culture of Education. Cambridge, MA. Harvard University Press.

Bunnell, T., 2010. The international baccalaureate and a framework for class consciousness: the potential outcomes of a class-for-itself. Discourse Stud. Cult. Polit. Educ. 31 (3), 351–361.

Butler, D.L., Winne, P.H., 1995. Feedback and self-regulated learning: a theoretical synthesis. Rev. Educ. Res. 65 (99), 245–281.

Campbell, J., 1971. Portable Jung. Penguin, London.

Carpentier, V., Pachler, N., Evans, K., Daly, C., 2011. Work-Learn-Educate: the WLE centre for excellence's conceptualisation of work-based learning. High. Educ. Skills Work-based Learn. 1 (3), 216–230.

Chavez, R.A., 2004. On the neurobiology of the creative process. Bull. Psychol. Arts 5, 29–35.

Coulby, D., 2000. Beyond the National Curriculum: School Knowledge and Society in the UK and Europe. RoutledgeFalmer, London.

Collins, A., Brown, J., Newman, S., 1989. Cognitive apprenticeship: teaching the crafts of reading, writing, and mathematics. In: Resnick, L.B. (Ed.), Knowing, Learning, and Instruction: Essays in Honour of Robert Glaser. Lawrence Erlbaum Associates, Hillsdale, NJ, pp. 453–494.

Connel, J.P., Kubish, A.C., 1998. Applying a theory of change approach to the evaluation of comprehensive community initiatives: progress, prospects and problems. In: Fulbright-Anderson, A., Kubish, A.C., Connel, J.P. (Eds.), New approaches to Evaluating Community Initiatives: Theory, Measurement and Analysis. Aspen Institute, Washington, DC.

Cordasco, F., 1976. A Brief History of Education: A Handbook of Information on Greek, Roman, Medieval, Renaissance, and Modern Educational Practice. Rowman & Littlefield, Maryland.

Cuban, L., 1986. Teachers and Machines. The Classroom Use of Technology Since 1920. Teachers College Press, New York.

Deutsch, K.W., Markovits, A.S., Platt, J., 1986. Advances in the Social Sciences, 1900–1980: What, Who, Where, How. Abt Books, Cambridge (Mass.).

Dewey, J., 1944. Democracy and Education. Macmillan Company, New York.

Dodgson, M., Gann, D., 2010. Innovation, A Very Short Introduction. Oxford University Press, Oxford.

Dodgson, M., Gann, D., Salter, A., 2005. Think, Play, Do. Technology, Innovation, and Organization. Oxford University Press, Oxford.

Duncker, K., 1945. On problem-solving. Psychol. Monogr. 58 (Whole No. 5).

Ellington, H., Race, P., 1994. Producing Teaching Material: A Handbook for Teachers and Trainers. Kogan Page Limited, London.

Engell, J., 1981. The Creative Imagination: Enlightenment to Romanticism. Cambridge (Mass.). Harvard University Press.

Evans, K., Guile, D., Harris, J., Allan, H., 2010. Putting knowledge to work: a new approach. Nurse Educ. Today 30 (3), 245–251.

Evans, K., Guile, D., Harris, J., 2011. Rethinking work-based learning –for education professionals who educate. In: Malloch, M., Cairns, L., Evan, K., O'Connor, B. (Eds.), The SAGE Handbook of Workplace Learning. Sage, London.

Falchikov, N., 2001. Learning Together: Peer Tutoring in Higher Education. RoutledgeFalmer, London.

Febvre, L., Martin, H., 1958. L'apparition du Livre. Les Éditions Albin Michel, Paris.

Feder, T., 2011. Brazil aims for its science to have greater impact. Phys. Today 26–28, September issue.

Fogarty, R., 1994. The Mindful School: How to Integrate the Curricula. Corwin, Thousand Oaks, CA.

Fomel, S., Claerbout, J.F., 2009. Guest editor's introduction, reproducible research. Comput. Sci. Eng. 11 (1), 5–7.

Foster, J.C., 1972. Independent Study: A Philosophical and Historical Analysis with Implications for the Technological Society. Catholic University of America, Washington, DC.

Freire, P., 1972. Cultural Action for Freedom. Penguin, Hardomsworth.

Gagne, R., 1985. The Condition of Learning. Holt, Rinehart and Winston, New York.

Gardiner, Eileen, Musto, R.G., 2010. The electronic book. In: Suarez, M.F., Woudhuysen, H.R. (Eds.), The Oxford Companion to the Book. Oxford University Press, Oxford, p. 164.

Gibbons, M., Limoges, C., Nowotny, H., Schwartzman, S., 1994. The New Production of Knowledge: The Dynamics of Science and Research in Contemporary Societies. Sage, Stockholm.

Glucksberg, S., 1962. The influence of strength of drive on functional fixedness and perceptual recognition. J. Exp. Psychol. 63, 36–41.

Goddard, B., 2012. Making a difference: Australian international education. UNSW Press, Sydney.

Godin, B., 2008. Innovation, the History of a Category. Project on the Intellectual History of Imitation. Working Paper No. 1, INRS, Quebec.

Habermas, J., 1987. The Philosophical Discourse of Modernity: Twelve Lectures. The MIT Press, Cambridge, Boston.

Hamel, G., Prahalad, C.K., 1994. Competing for the Future. Harvard Business School Press, Boston, MA.

Harris, K.R., Graham, S., 1992. Self-regulated development: a part of the writing process. In: Pressley, M., Harris, K.R., Guthrie, J. (Eds.), Promoting Academic Competence and Literacy in School. Academic Press, New York, pp. 277–309.

Harris, N., Gorard, S., 2009. Education policy, law and governance in the United Kingdom. Trends Bild. Int. 22 (S), 1–30.

Hattie, J., Timperley, H., 2007. The power of feedback. Rev. Educ. Res. 77 (1), 81–112.

Hmelo-Silver, C.E., 2004. Problem-based learning: what and how do students learn? Educ. Psychol. Rev. 16 (3), 235–266.

Illich, I., 1973. Deschooling Society. Penguin, Harmondsworth.

Keller, F.S., 1968. Good-bye teacher. J. Appl. Behav. Anal. 5, 79–89.

Kitzes, J., Peller, A., Goldfinger, S., Wackernagel, M., 2007. Current methods for calculating national ecological footprint accounts. Sci. Environ. Sustain. Soc. 4 (1), 1–9.

Knight, J., 1994. Internationalization: Elements and Checkpoints (Research Monograph, No. 7). Canadian Bureau for International Education, Ottawa, Canada.

Knowles, M.S., 1972. The Adult Learner: A Neglected Species. Gulf Pub. Co, Houston.

Kohlberg, L., 1981. Essays on Moral Development, Vol. I: The Philosophy of Moral Development. Harper & Row, San Francisco, CA.

Kolb, D.A., 1984. Experiential Learning Experience as a Source of Learning and Development. Prentice Hall, New Jersey.

Kop, R., 2011. The challenges to connectivism learning on open online networks: learning experiences during a massive open online course. Int. Rev. Res. Open Dist. Learn. 12 (3), 19–38.

Kysilka, M., 1998. Understanding integrated curriculum. Curr. J. 9, 197–209.

Landow, G.P., 1992. Hypertext: The Convergence of Contemporary Critical Theory and Technology. Johns Hopkins Press, Baltimore.

Lather, P., 1991. Getting Smart: Feminism Research and Pedagogy With/in the Postmodern. Routledge, London.

Laurillard, D., 2002. Rethinking University Teaching. A Conversational Framework for the Effective Use of Learning Technologies. Routledge, London.

Laurillard, D., 2008. Open teaching: the key to sustainable and effective open education. In: Iioshi, T., Vijay Kumar, M.S. (Eds.), Opening up Education: The Collective Advancement of Education Through Open Technology, Open Content, and Open Knowledge. MIT Press, Boston.

Laurillard, D., 2012. Teaching as a Design Science. Building Pedagogical Patterns for Learning and Technology. Routledge, New York.

Laurillard, D., McAndrew, P., 2009. TPD as online collaborative learning for innovation in teaching. In: Lindberg, O., Olofsson, A.D. (Eds.), Online Learning Communities and Teaching Professional Developments: Methods for Improved Educational Delivery. Springer, Berlin, pp. 230–246.

Levinson, R., Hand, M., Amos, R., 2008. A Research Study of the Perspectives on Science AS-level course (Report funded by UYSEG).

Lincoln, Y., Guba, E.G., 2000. The only generalization is: there is no generalization. In: Gomm, R., Hammerley, M., Foster, P. (Eds.), Case Study Method, Key Issues, Key Texts. Sage, London.

Lynch, J.P., 1972. Aristotle's School: A Study of a Greek Educational Institution. University of California, Print, Berkeley.

Machiavelli, N., 1953. Il Principe, Florence, Italy: Antonio Blado d'Asola. Translated by Harvey Mansfield as *The Prince*. Chicago: University of Chicago Press, 1985.

Maia, C., 2008. Work-based Learning: a nova geração do e-learning. Rev. Diálogo Educ. 8 (24), 459–472.

Marshall, J., 1990. Foucalt and Educational Research. In: Ball, S.J. (Ed.), Foucault and Education: Discipline and Knowledge. Routledge, London.

McAndrew, P., Goodyear, P., Dalziel, J., 2006. Patterns, designs and activities: unifying descriptions of learning structures. Int. J. Learn. Technol. 2 (2/3), 216–242.

Meece, J., Anderman, E., Anderman, L., 2006. Classroom goal structure, student motivation, and academic achievement. Ann. Rev. Psychol. 57 (1), 487–503.

Merril, D., 1983. Component display theory. In: Reigeluth, C.M. (Ed.), Instructional Design Theories and Models: An Overview of their Current States. Lawrence Erlbaum, Hillsdale, NJ.

Mezirow, J., 1991. Transformative Dimensions of Adult Learning. Jossey-Bass, San Francisco.

Moore, A., 2012. Teaching and Learning: Pedagogy, Curriculum and Culture. Routledge, London.

Mota, R., 2007. Educação Superior: Assunto de Estado e Prioridade Social. Ensino Superior Particular Brasileiro, 287–295.

Mota, R., 2008. A universidade Aberta do Brasil. In: Litto, Fredric, Formiga, Manoel (Eds.), Educação a Distância: O Estado da Arte. Pearson Prentice Hall, São Paulo, pp. 297–303.

Mota, R., 2009a. Inovação tecnológica: desafios e perspectivas. Educação Brasileira 31, 61–80.

Mota, R., 2009b. Novos Tempos, Espaços e Públicos: Os Complexos Desafios da Educação Superior no Brasil. Interesse Nacional 2, 77–87.

Mota, R., 2011. O Papel da Inovação na Sociedade e na Educação. In: Colombo, Sonia, Rodrigues, Gabriel M. (Eds.), Desafios da Sociedade Contemporânea. ARTMED, Porto Alegre, pp. 459–474.

Mota, R., 2013. Exploring Integrated Independent Learning and Innovation in the Brazilian Postgraduate Programmes. Revista Brasileira de Pós-Graduação/CAPES 10 (20), 289–312.

Mota, R., Chaves, H., 2006. Universidade Aberta do Brasil e Perspectivas da Educação a Distância no Brasil. Educação on Line (Org. Marcos Silva). Edições Loyola, São Paulo, pp. 459–474.

Mota, R., Martins, R.O., 2008. A Política do MEC para Educação Superior e Ensino de Engenharia no Brasil. Revista de Ensino de Engenharia 27, 52–68.

Mota, R., Flores, R.Z., Sepel, L., Loreto, E., 2003. Método Científico e Fronteiras do Conhecimento. CESMA Edições, Santa Maria-RS.

Mulgan, G., Rushanara, A., Halkett, R., Sanders, B., 2007. In and Out of Sync: The Challenge of Growing Social Innovations. National Endowment for Science, Technology and the Arts (NESTA), London.

Newman, W., 2011. Technology and alchemical debate in the late middle ages. Isis 80 (3), 423–445.

Pachler, N., Daly, C., 2011. Key issues in e-Learning Research and Practice. Continuum, London.

Pear, J.J., Crone-Todd, D.E., 1999. Personalized system of instruction is cyberspace. J. Appl. Behav. Anal. 32, 205–209.

Pedersen, O., 1997. The First Universities: Studium Generale and the Origins of University Education in Europe. Cambridge UP, Print, Cambridge.

Philips, D., Schweisfurth, M., 2008. Comparative and International Education: An Introduction to Theory, Method, and Practice. Continuum International Publishing Group, London.

Piaget, J., 1952. The Origins of Intelligence in Children. W.W. Norton & Co, New York, NY, US.

Pink, D.H., 2009. Drive: The Surprising Truth about What Motivates Us. Riverhead Books, New York.

Pintrich, P., Schunk, D., 1996. Motivation in Education: Theory, Research & Applications. Prentice-Hall, Englewood Cliffs, NJ.

Prober, C.G., Heat, C., 2012. Lectures halls without lectures. A proposal for medical education. N. Engl. J. Med. 366 (18), 1657–1679.

Santos, A.I., 2011. Open Educational Resources in Brazil. State-of-the-Art, Challenges and Prospects for Development and Innovation. Report UNESCO-Institute for Information Technologies in Education. Printed in Russia Federation.

Scott, D., Watson, D., Walter, C., Hughes, G., Evans, C., Burke, P., 2012. Learning Transitions in Higher Education. Palgrave, London.

Scott, D., Lunt, I., Thorne, L., Brown, A., 2004. Professional Doctorates: Integrating Professional and Academic Knowledge. Open University Press, Buckingham, pp. 187.

Scott, P., 2000. Higher Education Re-formed. Falmer Press, London.

Schuller, T., Watson, D., 2009. Learning Through Life: Inquiry into the Future for Lifelong Learning. National Institute of Adult Continuing Education, Leicester.

Schumpeter, J.A., 1939. Business Cycles: A Theoretical, Historical, and Statistical Analysis of the Capitalism Process. McGraw-Hill, New York.

Schumpeter, J.A., 1961. The theory of economic development: an inquiry into profits, capital, credit, interest, and business cycle. Translated from German by Redvers Opie. Oxford University Press, New York.

Seliger, G., Him, H.-G., Kernbaum, S., 2008. Approaches to sustainable manufacturing. Int. J. Sustain. Manuf. 1 (1/2), 58–77.

Selwyn, N., 2011. Education and Technology. Key Issues and Debates. Continuum Int. Publ. Group, London.

Sharma, P., Hannafin, M., 2007. Scaffolding in technology-enhanced learning environments. Interact. Learn. Environ. 15 (1), 27–46.

Siemens, G., 2005. Connectivism: a learning theory for a digital age. Int. J. Ins.l Technol. Dist. Learn. 2 (1), 3–10.

Skinner, B.F., 1938. The Behavior of Organisms: An Experimental Analysis. Appleton-Century, Oxford, England.

Sockalingam, N., Rotgans, J., Schmidt, H.G., 2011. Student and tutor perceptions on attributes of effective problems in problem-based learning. High. Educ. 62 (1), 1–16.

Spellings, M., 2006. A Test of Leadership. Charting the Future of US Higher Education. Education Publications Center, U.S. Department of Education, Jessup, MD.

Suh, N.P., 2010. A Theory of Innovation and Case Study. Int. J. Innov. Manag. 14, 893–913.

Taylor, J., 2012. Think Again. Continuum Books, London.

Teles, A., Joia, L.A., 2012. Digital inclusion (infoinclusion) in Piraí digital: empirical evidence based on the actor-network theory. J. Inf. Technol. Manag. 9 (2), 369–390.

Torrance, E.P., Safter, H.P., 1999. Making the Creative Leap Beyond. Creative Education Foundation Press, Buffalo, NY.

Torrance, H., Pryor, J., 1998. Formative Assessment: Teaching, Learning and Assessment in the Classroom. Open University Press, Buckingham.

Van de Pol, J., Volman, M., Beishuizen, J., 2010. Scaffolding in teacher−student interaction: a decade of research. Educ. Psychol. Rev. 1−26.

Vygotsky, L.S., 1978. Mind and Society: The Development of Higher Mental Processes. Cambridge, MA. Harvard University Press.

Wolf, M., 2007. Proust and the Squid: The Story and Science of the Reading Brain. Harper Perennial, New York.

Wood, D., Wood, H., 1996a. Contingency in tutoring and learning. Learn. Instr. 6 (4), 391−397.

Wood, D., Wood, H., 1996b. Vygotsky, tutoring and learning. Oxford Rev. Educ. 22 (1), 5−16.

Yeager, D.S., Walton, G.M., 2011. Social-psychological interventions in education: they're not magic. Rev. Educ. Res. 81, 267−301.

Yeatman, A., 1990. Bureaucrats, Femocrats, Technocrats: Essays on the Contemporary Australian State. Allen & Unwin, Australia.

Yemini, M., 2012. Internationalization assessment in schools: theoretical contributions and practical implications. J. Res. Int. Educ. 11 (2), 152−164.

Youtiea, J., Shapira, P., 2008. Building an innovation hub: a case study of the transformation of university roles in regional technological and economic development. Res. Policy 37, 1188−1204.

Zimmernan, B., Schunk, D., 2011. Handbook of Self-regulation of Learning and Performance. Routledge, New York.

Zimmerman, B.J., 2002. Becoming a self-regulated learner: an overview. Theory Into. Pract. 41 (2), 64−72.

# INDEX

*Note*: Page numbers followed by "*f*" and "*t*" refers to figures and tables respectively.

## A
Acceleration and turn-over, 137–139
Alexander the Great, 46–48
Amazon Kindle, 69
ANPROTEC, 35–36
Apple iPad, 69
Area Training Organizations (ATOs), 129–130
Aristotle, 46, 48
   peripatetic school, 47
Artificial disciplinary boundaries, 60
Assessment for learning, 54, 79, 143–144
   convergent assessment, 79–80
   divergent assessment, 79–80
Autonomy in learning, 54

## B
*Banco Garantia*, 113–114
Behaviourism, 81
Behaviourist meta-theory, 81–82, 84
Bio-prospecting service, 110–111
Book, 48–50
Brazil, 1, 9–15
   C.E.S.A.R., 104–107
   case studies in, 97
   Ease of Doing Business rank, 36
   education in, 8–19
   Engineering, Education and Entrepreneurship, 104–107
   higher education institutions in, 11–12
   innovation strategies in, 34–37
   Lemann Center for Educational Entrepreneurship And Innovation, 113–116
   Piraí Digital Project, 101–104
   school curriculum in, 59–60
   start-up neoprospecta, 109–113
   Veduca educational experiment, 107–109
Brazilian Federal Agency for Support and Evaluation of Postgraduate Education (CAPES), 13
British Broadcast Corporation (BBC), 112, 126–127
Bruner, Jerome, 76

## C
C.E.S.A.R., 104–107
Candle problem, 52–53
CensoEAD.BR, 108
Coaching model, 85
Cognitivism, 59–60, 84
Colleges (*Centros Universitários*), in Brazil, 11–12
Computer-aided design (CAD), 134–135
Computers, in learning process, 65, 69, 76, 101–102
Concept-formation focus, 87
Concept of innovation, 21–25, 140–141
Connected curriculum, 122
Constructivism, 84–85
Content management, 51–52
ContentSense, 109
Creative economies, 2, 24, 140–141
Creativity and innovation, 57–58, 139–142
Criticality, 55
Critical perspective, 26, 29
Curricular modes, in continuum, 124*f*
Curriculum matters, 58–61
   in Brazil, 59–60
   in England, 59–60

## D
Democratizing innovation, 2, 24, 140–141
Dialogic confrontation, 124
Digital technologies, 2–3, 50–54, 58–59, 64, 145
   in Brazil, 107–108
   in England, 131
   teaching and learning approaches, 90–93
Digital theory of learning, 73
Disciplinarity, 55
Disciplinary forms of knowledge, 24–25, 55, 138
Discovery, 23, 112–113
   vs invention, 23
Dispositionality, 55
Dispositional learning, 54
Dogmatic instruction, 73–75
Duncker, Karl, 52–53

## E

Ease of Doing Business rank, in Brazil, 36
E-book (electronic book), 68–69
Edison, Thomas, 58–59
Educational revolution, 2, 41
  book, 48–50
  digital technologies, 50–54
  first, 48
  principal characteristics, 44t
  school, 43–48
  second, 41
  third, 41
EMBRAPA, 37
Emerging economies, 34–35
Engineering, Education and Entrepreneurship, 104–107
England
  case studies in, 117
  education in, 8–19
  Imperial College London, 133–135
  innovation strategies in, 37–40
  Rugby School, 120–126
  school curriculum in, 59–60
  teaching Shakespeare at Stratford-upon-Avon, 117–120
  Team Engineering at Open University (OU), 126–129
  word-based learning at institute of education, 129–133
Enquiry-based learning (EBL), 125–126
  mode of learning, 125–126
Epistemic framework, 26
E-portfolios, 90
European Union (EU), 38–39
Expert credentialism, 73
Extrinsic motivation, 52

## F

Face-to-face learning environment, 90–91
Federal Government Financing Agency for Projects and Studies (FINEP), 35, 111
Federal Innovation Law (2004), 35–36
First educational revolutions, 41
  principal characteristics, 44t
Flexibility, 7, 82, 91, 93, 144–145
Fragmented curriculum, 122
Fundação Estudar, 114

## G

Gann, David, 133
General Certificate of Secondary Education (GCSE), 15

General National Vocational Qualifications (GNVQs), 16–17
Goal clarity, 85–86
Good Will Law (2005), 35–36
Grasset, Eugene, 21, 22f
Greeks, education method, 48
Gutenberg, Johann, 48–49, 69

## H

Higher Education Funding Council for England (HEFCE), 131
Higher education institutions in Brazil, 11–12
Human Development Index (HDI), 26
HyperTextual model, 50–51, 145

## I

Illich, Ivan, 65
Imagination
  association-integration stage, 57–58
  elaboration stage, 58
Imperial College London, 3, 133–135
Incremental innovation, 22–23
Individual self-discovery, 73
Infodev, 35–36
Innovation, 1, 21
  concept, 21–25
  creativity and, 139–142
  and education, 1–3, 55
    curriculum matters, 58–61
    Massive Open Online Course (MOOC), 65–68
    teachers as designers, 61–65
    teaching for innovation, 68–70
  features of, 57
  and independent learning, 89–90, 131, 141–142
  vs invention, 23–24
  knowledge-development, 26–31
  strategies in Brazil, 34–37
  strategies in England, 37–40
  and sustainability, 25–26
  teaching for, 68–70
  technological, 6
  types of, 23–24
Innovation technology (IvT), 133–134
Instruction, 54, 87
Integrated curriculum, 123
International Baccalaureate (IB) Foundation, 7
International education, 1–2
Internationalization
  in education, 5–7
  in higher education, 6–7

Internet, 3, 127, 137–138
Interpersonal domain, 59–60
Interpretivism, 26–28
Intrapersonal domain, 59–60
Intrinsic motivation, 52
Invention
   of digital technologies, 50–51, 145
   vs discovery, 23
   vs innovation, 23–24
   of paper, 49

## J
Janus-faced model, 25

## K
Keller, Fred S., 81–82
Keller method, 81–82
KeyNews, 109
Khan Academy, 92–93
Knowledge, 60, 125–127, 137–139, 144
   -construction, 24–25
      process, 55
   -development, 26–31
      and innovation, 31–34
      management scheme, 33$f$
      modes, 24–25, 55
   management, 51–52
   production, 55
Kohlberg, Lawrence, 41–42
Kolb, David, 87–88

## L
Laurillard's Conversational Framework, 63–64
Learning, 1, 45–46, 64–65, 74–76, 125
   assessment for, 54
   autonomy in, 54
   in Brazil, 97
   and capacity development, 140–143
   computational view of, 78
   digital approaches, 90–93
   by doing, 74
   e-learning, 132
   in England, 117, 119
   environments, 80–81, 144
   events, in life course, 42
   face-to-face, 91
   frameworks, 81–85
   independent, 89–90
   life-long, 74
   mobile, 132
   peer, 86

   as process, 2–3, 53, 75–76
   service, 74
   sets/sequences, 85–89
   skills, 94
      cognitive skills, 94
      metacognitive, 94
      motivational capacity, 94
      pedagogic, 94
      persistence, 94
      preparation, 94
   technologies, 1, 52
   theories, 54, 76–81
   traditional approaches, 41
   transition, 41–42
   in virtual environment, 91
   work-based, 129–133
Learning Cycle, 87–88
Lemann Center for Educational Entrepreneurship and Innovation, 113–116
Life course, 41–42
Life-long learning, 74
"*L'image du Monde*" 4$f$
London Day Training College (LDTC), 129–130
London Mobile Learning Group (LMLG), 132
Low-cost networking technologies, 103
"The Lyceum" 46–47

## M
Marketing innovation, 2, 24, 140–141
Massachusetts Institute of Technology (MIT), 66, 74–75
Massive Open Online Course (MOOC), 65–68
Mentoring, 86
Meta-cognition, 59–60, 88
Meta-comprehension, 88
Meta-memory, 88
Mobile learning, 132
Models of learning, 54
Modern printed book, 48–50
Motivation, 52

## N
National Centre for Excellence in Teaching and Learning Languages (CETL), 131
Neoprospecta, 110–113
Nested curriculum, 122
Networked curriculum, 123–124
Normalization and individualization, 138

## O

Observation, 85
Office for Standards in Education (OFSTED), 18
On-going training, 90
Online lectures, 92–93
Open innovation, 2, 24, 140–141
Open University (OU), Team Engineering at, 126–129
Organizational innovation, 2, 24, 140–141
Organization for Economic Cooperation and Development (OECD), 32

## P

Paper, invention of, 49
Pedagogical approach, principles of, 61–62, 73–75
Peer learning, 86
Peer-mentoring scheme, 90
Personalized System of Instruction (PSI), 81–82
Piaget, Jean, 41–42
Piraí Digital Project, 101–104
Plato, 45–46, 48
Policy borrowing, 8–9
Portability, 91, 144–145
Porto Digital, 104–105
Positivism/empiricism, 26–27
Postmodernism, 26, 28
Power strategies, 138
Practice, defined, 88
Practicum learning, 74
Problem-solving pedagogy, 88
"Putting Knowledge to Work" (PKTW), 132

## R

Radical compression, 137–138
Radio, as educational technology, 58–59
Rafaello Sanzio's painting, 43–45, 45f
Reflection, 87–88
Reform processes, in education, 146–148
　professional development model, 147
　quasi-market model, 147
　social participation model, 147–148
　top-down model, 146–147
Relocation of power, 138
Resources, defined, 42
Royal Shakespeare Company (RSC), 118–119
Rugby School, 120–126
　Perspective on Science, 121–122

## S

School, invention of, 43–48
School of Athens, 43–45, 45f
Schools (*Faculdades*), in Brazil, 11–12
Schumpeter, Joseph, 23
Science and religion, 56–57
Science-technology-innovation model, 33f
　time-sequence traditional model, 33f
Scott, Peter, 137
　late-modern world, features of, 137
Second educational revolutions, 41
　principal characteristics, 44t
Self-regulated learning, 89, 141–142
Self-regulation, 88
Service learning, 74
Shakespeare, William, 117
Siemens, George, 68
Simulation, defined, 87
Skinner, B.F., 81
Small Business Research Initiative (SBRI), 38
Social innovation, 24
Socrates, 43–45
Socratic method, 43–45, 73–74
Start-up neoprospecta, 109–113
Stepped system of learning events, 42
Stepped system of learning markers, 41–42
Stepped system of resource accumulations, 42
Stepped system of statuses, 41–42
Stobart, J.C., 126–127
Study skills session, 90
Sustainability, 25–26, 112–113
Symbol-processing, 76–77, 84

## T

Teachers as designers, 61–65
Teaching for innovation, 68–70
Teaching Shakespeare at Stratford-upon-Avon, 117–120
Team Engineering at Open University (OU), 126–129
Technical rationality, 55
Technological innovation, 6, 22–23, 140–141
Text books, 58–59
Theory of learning, 3, 54, 75, 90–91, 142
Threaded curriculum, 123
Traditional teaching and learning approaches, 41
Trans-disciplinary forms of knowledge, 24–25, 55
Transferability, 91, 145

## U

United Nations Development Programme, 139–140
United Nations Educational, Scientific and Cultural Organization (UNESCO), 5
Universidade de São Paulo (USP), 12–13
Universidade Estadual de Campinas (Unicamp), 12–13
Universidade Federal de Minas Gerais, 13
Universidade Federal de São Paulo, 13
Universidade Federal do Rio de Janeiro, 13
Universidad Nacional Autónoma de México (UNAM), 12–13
Universities (Universidades), in Brazil, 11–12
Universities, changing role of, 137

## V

Veduca educational experiment, 107–109
Virtual learning environment, 91, 144–145
  meta-cognitive progress, 93
  portability, 91
  storage and retrieval facilities, 93
  student autonomy, 92
  transferability, 91
Vygotskian framework, 78, 143

## W

Webbed curriculum, 123
Web-enabled smart phones, 132–133
Wedgwood, Josiah, 117
Word-based learning at institute of education, 129–133
Work-based Learning for Educational Professionals Centre (WLE), 131
World Bank, 35–36
World Competitiveness Yearbook (WCY), 34–35
World Economic Forum, (WEF), 39
World Wide Web, 50–51, 93

www.ingramcontent.com/pod-product-compliance
Lightning Source LLC
Chambersburg PA
CBHW071400290426
44108CB00014B/1625